AUS
FOR T

The Traveler's Guide to Make The Most Out of Your Trip to Australia- Where to Go, Eat, Sleep & Party

By Dagny Taggart

Disclaimer

The information provided in this book is designed to provide helpful information on the subjects discussed. The author's books are only meant to provide the reader with the basics travel guidelines of a certain location, without any warranties regarding the accuracy of the information and advice provided. Each traveler should do their own research before departing.

Table of Contents

CHAPTER 3: IMMERSING YOURSELF IN AUSTRALIA 34

CHAPTER 4: AN OVERVIEW OF THE DESTINATION CHAPTERS 39

CHAPTER 5: SYDNEY AND AROUND...41

CHAPTER 6: MELBOURNE AND VICTORIA 48

Dedicated to those who love going beyond their own frontiers.

Keep on traveling,

Dagny Taggart

My FREE Gift to You!

As a way of saying thank you for downloading my book, I'd like to send you an exclusive gift that will revolutionize the way you learn new languages. It's an extremely comprehensive PDF with 15 language hacking rules that **will help you learn 300% <u>faster</u>, with <u>less effort</u>, and with <u>higher than ever retention rates</u>**.

This guide is an amazing complement to the book you just got, and could easily be a stand-alone product, but for now I've decided to give it away for free, to thank you for being such an awesome reader, and to make sure I give you all the value that I can to help you succeed faster on your language learning journey.

To get your FREE gift, go to the link below, follow the steps, and I'll send it to your email address right away.

>> <u>http://bitly.com/Language-Gift</u> <<

GET **INSTANT** ACCESS

Learn Any Language 300% FASTER

>> Get Full Online Language Courses With Audio Lessons <<

Would you like to learn a new language before you start your trip? I think that's a great idea. Now, why don't you do it 300% *FASTER*?

I've partnered with the most revolutionary language teachers to bring you the very language online courses I've ever seen. It's a mind-blowing program specifically created for language hackers such as ourselves. It will allow you learn ANY language, from French to Chinese, 3x faster, straight from the comfort of your own home, office, or wherever you may be. It's like having an unfair advantage!

You can choose from a wide variety of languages, such as French, Spanish, Italian, German, Chinese, Portuguese, and A TON more.

Each Online Course consists of:

+ 91 Built-In Lessons
+ 33 Interactive Audio Lessons
+ 24/7 Support to Keep You Going

The program is extremely engaging, fun, and easy-going. You won't even notice you are learning a complex foreign language from scratch. And before you realize it, by the time you go through all the lessons you will officially become a truly solid speaker.

Old classrooms are a thing of the past. It's time for a revolution.

If you'd like to go the extra mile, follow the link below, and let the revolution begin

>>http://www.bitly.com/foreign-language-courses<<

CHECK OUT THE COURSE »

Introduction
Why You Will Fall In Love With Australia

Australia lingers long in every impression. From burning red desert to bustling metropolis, aboriginal lifestyles to surf culture, the land down under seems to serve up a feast of preconceptions. This vast island, cast adrift in the South Pacific, seems to ignite the imagination unlike anywhere else. Australia. Just picture it and it's impossible to focus on a single image; Sydney, Uluru, the Great Barrier Reef, the desert, the beach, everything in between. We'll let you into a little secret. All that dreaming, all that unadulterated reverie of Australia...it's pretty much exactly what Australia is like when you visit.

Let's indulge a little on the country's appeal. Over 20,000 miles of virtually untouched coastline, a series of cities founded on ingenuity and intrigue, endemic wildlife skipping around all over... This is where you'll find the world's biggest monolith, it's longest reef, oldest rainforest, longest surviving culture, and a completely new definition of uninhabited wilderness. With Australia, there's never a debate about whether you want to go. It's hard to find a soul on the planet who isn't inspired by the thought of this immense island nation.

The question is more about how to transform Australia from fantasy to reality. First up are the practicalities. Just flying across the country takes five hours, nothing but scorched landscape beneath the wingtips. Even on the ever popular East Coast you can drive for hours without seeing anything but sugar plantations and the odd kangaroo. Second up is cost. Australia's transformation from rugged hinterland into sophisticated nation knows no boundaries, and the spiraling costs have many visitors surviving off boxed wine and jam sandwiches. Finally, there's the dilemma of finding time. Such a vast far flung destination deserves oodles of time. So what can realistically be squeezed into an itinerary if you don't have three months to spare?

Consider the three questions and Australia can easily be left to rot in the annals of travel daydreams. But as the Aussies would say, no worries. The locals' serene and easygoing attitude forms the paradigm for this guidebook. There's no need to completely overthink Australia. This is an indelibly easy country to travel in and this guidebook believes in giving you all the information and tools to turn a dream trip into reality. All the core practicalities are considered, helping you plan an itinerary regardless of how much time you have to spend. Costs are outlined, along with numerous ways to reduce them without reliving days of being a squalid student.

This guidebook is about all the essential information you need to plan and realize a trip to Australia. Because once you've got it planned the country will do the rest. So jump forward into a nation of superlatives, into a mesmerizing concoction of escapism and adventure. Some people say that Australia is a country for finding yourself. We prefer to think it's a country for getting lost, amidst the finest landscapes and experiences on the planet.

Sydney Opera House: As iconic as it gets.

Chapter 1
Welcome to Australia!

Australia at a glance

Let's start with the obvious. Australia is huge. It's also vastly unpopulated, a handful of cities containing the large bulk of a 25 million population. This is a place of wilderness and hinterland, a dry and barren land that evokes all the impressions of desert and the bush. Traveling between destinations almost always takes a day, even if you're flying, yet arrive for just a week and there's plenty to discover with a realistic plan. Sandwiched between desert and ocean is a thin coastline of development and greenery, home to the iconic cities and more deserted sand than you could ever possibly imagine.

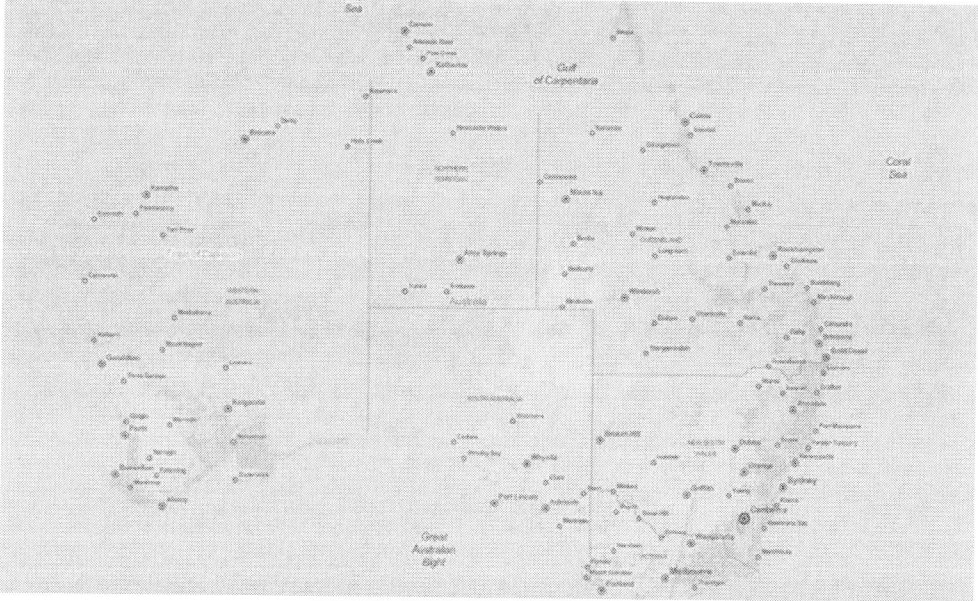

The East Coast is more developed with Sydney and Melbourne providing the most popular entry points to the country. Most visitors stay east, traversing the renowned wonders that dot a long coastline, including the Great Barrier Reef and Whitsunday Islands. South of the two famous cities but still firmly on the eastern side, you'll find the Southern Coast and island of Tasmania. The West Coast is far less developed, save for the rapidly expanding and beautiful city of Perth. Journeys here are more off the beaten track, the intrepid coastline a place for real adventure. The red center is exactly that, a vast red desert where you can drive 1000 miles without seeing another person or building. It's achingly authentic, but can be brutal and unpleasant for the unprepared.

Land in a city and you'd be forgiven for an immediately blinding by the lights. Australia can be as developed and futuristic as anywhere in the world. However, at its heart, the country retains the tranquil atmosphere of days gone by. Even the Sydney city slickers will jump off work early for a surf. Settling into the local rhythm happens almost instantaneously; expect to be gently rolling on an anything-is-possible mentality. Not in an American Dream kind of way. Think instead, that if anything is possible, then there's time for a beer in the meantime. Australia and Aussies are fun, always focused on absorbing the best of life and having a laugh. You can't help but smile, especially with the endless days of sunshine, exuberant coating of nature, and encompassing wonder that seems to cascade from the hotel window.

Australia's tourist infrastructure matches its modern world status. Roads are in excellent condition, flights connect remote destinations, and the range of accommodation always impresses with its quality. Arrive in the most far-flung destination and there will be a tour company offering some kind of unique trip. Just to get you excited, here are a few examples:

Iconic Experiences

- **Sydney** is surrounded by green, dissected by a river, and fringed by memorable surf. Yet it's also a marvelous blend of ultra plush development and old-world ambiance, one that's stuffed with iconic sights and must-see landmarks. (See Chapter 5: Sydney and Around).

- The wild **West Coast** is a place for beach dreamers, for those that imagine thousands of miles of sand without a single footprint. Jump out into the Indian Ocean and tropical marine worlds serve up kaleidoscopic beauty, like swimming with whale sharks in **Ningaloo**. (See Chapter 11: The West Coast)

A koala in Victoria.

- **Kangaroos and koalas** feature highly on all postcard images of Australia, yet few can picture how closely they merge with urbanity. Just outside the colorful artistic streets of **Melbourne** you can spot hundreds of marsupials thriving in their natural habitat. (See Chapter 6: Melbourne and Victoria).

- Visible from space and stretching half way down the **East Coast**, the **Great Barrier Reef** needs little introduction. Yet for all the boasting about size, there's a wonderful intimacy to exploring its colors and weirdness. (See Chapter 9: The East Coast).

- Running between Melbourne and Adelaide, the **Great Ocean Road** is perhaps the country's most dramatic expanse of cliff lines and sandy havens, the bays interluded by staggering rocky pinnacles that stand isolated in the water (See Chapter 6: Melbourne and Victoria).

- Peculiar **Tasmania** runs with its own style, the island's geography more reminiscent of nearby New Zealand than the mainland. It's a place for outdoor adventures, wild camping, and the most laid-back characters around (See Chapter 8: Tasmania).

- **Kangaroo Island** isn't just home to the hopping version of marsupials, it's one of the final utopias for koalas. Expect to find almost all Australia's endemic wildlife without even having to leave your chalet balcony (See Chapter 7: South Australia).

- It's just a rock. But what a rock! Towering above the desert, burning red **Uluru** is the world's largest monolith. Yet it's far more than aesthetic fancy, this is the heartbeat of aboriginal culture and a genuine journey into remote desert. (See Chapter 10: The Red Center).

Unique Experiences

- Explore the seemingly endless hinterland of **Kakadoo National Park**, an evocative mix of desert and green in the north of Australia's red center. (See Chapter 10: The Red Center).

- Cruise through the elegant vineyards of the **Barossa Valley**, Australia's premier wine destination rolling with picturesque backdrops and long days of sensual tasting (See Chapter 7: South Australia).

- Stand on the very eastern edge of Australia at **Byron Bay**, the high rugged cliffs looking out onto breaching whales and other marine beauties (see Chapter 9: The East Coast).

- Gaze out onto the mystical haze of the **Blue Mountains**, the surreal color juxtaposed with a rich canopy of eucalyptus trees and some sublime hiking trails (see Chapter 5: Sydney and Around).

- Hire a car and drive **south of Perth**, the Indian Ocean coastline completely deserted and filled with untamed surfing spots. You can drive for miles and see nothing but pristine beach awaiting your footprints (see Chapter 11: The West Coast).

- Tasmania is 45% **national park** and its free to camp almost everywhere. So lace up the hiking boots and find a sublime piece of nature beneath the stars (See Chapter 8: Tasmania).

- Wander the **Melbourne riverside** and soak up the atmosphere of a city priding itself on art and culture; buskers, street artists, colonial relics standing over eclectic gourmet restaurants, and a treasure found down every side street (See Chapter 6: Melbourne and Victoria).

The world's oldest living rainforest, Daintree on the East Coast (chapter 9)

How to Use This Guide

This guidebook is split up into three distinct sections, each building on the last and offering a thorough impression of Australia. You're not going to find page after page of individual hotel listings or information what to eat on a Tuesday night in Airlie beach. This planning guide provides everything you need to plan and make your dream trip a reality. Australia is about getting lost so there's no need to concoct an hourly itinerary. However, arrive without a plan and this huge country can feel scarily inaccessible. So we stick to the essential information and ensure you can soak up the indelible local style and maximize the fun.

At the same time, this guidebook should be all you need to travel Australia. This is a remarkably easy country to travel in. English is the local language (albeit with a few twangs of indecipherable slang), tourists are always well catered for, and chatting with strangers is just what you do. Use this guidebook to plan your trip and everything else will take care of itself. If it's important then we've included it. If it's not, then it didn't make the cut. Australia is far too good a country to waste pages listing below par restaurants or experiences that blitz the credit card for nothing in return.

Chapter 2 provides all the basics on Australia. It's about how to get around, where to sleep, how to get good value and limit your costs, and all the basics for planning potential routes. It's the country in a nutshell, a quick fire run through what's important before you travel. Importantly, it answers the three questions that inhibit most Australian travel dreams: practicalities, cost, and time.

Chapter 3 focuses on how to fully immersive yourself in the Australian experience. It covers culture and tradition, from what they drink in the pub to the languages spoke by Aboriginal tribes. Having some form of Australian mindset elevates the experience from postcard image to real travel experience. Yes, Australia is full of seemingly must-see sights and you've already probably got a list in your head. But the country's unique appeal also lies in the atmosphere that pervades throughout. Chapter 3 helps ensure that you're fully braced to go on walkabout and shout "fair dinkem" when it all works out.

Chapters 4 – 11 offer detailed information about destinations in Australia and how they can be worked into a realistic itinerary. Australia is a huge country yet it doesn't have many roads or airports, so planning a route is easier that you might expect. Each chapter is self-contained and moves in a geographical order, meaning that it's easily explorable on its own. It's also a link with other chapters for those planning wider Australia trips. With each chapter you're introduced to the region and the travel practicalities, then individual destinations are detailed with a focus on the experiences and highlights.

Chapter 2
Planning Your Trip Ahead(Travel Routes, Itineraries, Etc)

Travel Routes and Itineraries

Route planning is easier that you might imagine in a country of this size. In essence, Australia has one coastal road that travels almost 20,000 miles around the country, and then a couple of barren roads that cross the desert. So you won't be encountering too many indecipherable crossroads. Virtually nobody has the time to cover it all on a single vacation, so your travel route and itinerary will depend on the airports that dot the country. Note that while some places look relatively close on the map, distances in Australia are huge. For example, Sydney to Melbourne is a 12 hour drive.

Each chapter of this travel guide is based around one or two entry airports. A wider network of flights then extends from these entry airports, connecting many remote dots. However, these remote airports are serviced by a small handful of flights, so you'll inevitably have to arrive from or depart to one of the larger airports below.

Entry Destinations

- Sydney – Largest entry airport and start or end point for longer trips along the East Coast.

- Melbourne – Tucked away in the south of the country. Used as a base to explore Victoria.

- Adelaide – Southern Australia entry point. Relatively small airport.

- Brisbane / Cairns – Airports in the center and north of the East Coast.

- Perth – Major airport and city on the West Coast.

- Ayer's Rock / Alice Springs / Darwin – Tourist focused airports in the red center with mainly domestic flights.

Classic Routes at a Glance

With one week: With one week, the best option is usually to combine two of the entry airports above, with three or four days in each exploring the surrounding area. The most popular choice is Sydney and Cairns.

With two weeks: Two main options. Choose three or four of the entry destinations and hop between them. Or hire a car and explore a part of the coastline with a one way trip. Cairns to Brisbane, Brisbane to Sydney, Sydney to Adelaide, or Perth to Broome.

With three weeks: Enough to fly across the country and pick a handful of destinations. There are numerous possibilities with the genuine chance to combine both East Coast and West Coast.

One month: Again, enough time to fly around the country. Also enough time for a serious road trip and just about long enough to travel Cairns down to Sydney on the East Coast. Don't overstretch yourself though. One month won't be long enough to see all of Australia.

Up to two months: For financial reasons, most choose to rent a vehicle for most of their trip, usually with a couple of flights to start or end the trip.

When To Go and Understanding Different Seasons

There's no prizes for guessing the mainstay of the Australian climate. A fierce sun rolls around a cloudless sky for almost the entire year. Australia is hot, and with a gaping ozone hole up above, it quickly dishes out discomfort for anyone unprepared. This is the country of desert and bush fires remember, so slap on the suncream and respect the lack of water. However, Australia stretches a few thousands latitudinal miles and there's a few anomalies that have to be considered. There's never a bad time to visit Australia, but the time of year will undoubtedly form part of your travel planning. Below is a very brief overview:

The color of the landscape should provide an indication to the weather.

The Hot Summer (December to Febuary)

Best for: Melbourne and South Australia.
Not as good for: The Red Center and the West Coast.

Summer is hot. Hot, hot, hot. Desert temperatures regularly stay above 100°F and the West Coast can become blisteringly dry. You'll be hard pressed to find a scrap of rain anywhere other than the tropical East Coast, a factor that entices people to Southern Australia and the cities of Sydney and Melbourne. There's many beach destinations that can fulfill classic images of postcard heaven at this time of year. The northern East Coast is hot all year round although it's more tropical in summer with regular downpours. Christmas and early January is peak season in the cities and prices can be astronomical.

The Cooler Half of the Year (May to September)

Best for: Just about everywhere, particularly the Red Center and East and West Coasts.
Not as good for: Melbourne and Tasmania.

The winter months bring a slight respite from the heat and the desert can now be explored at more manageable temperatures. The East Coast will have clearer skies and the West Coast also benefits from a slight dip in the mercury. Tropical East Coast is at peak season now. While Sydney has a mixed winter the weather isn't off-putting, but Melbourne and Tasmania have more European climates; grey skies and sub 60 temperatures aren't quite the image most people have of Australia. Also remember that you'll have two to four less daylight hours during winter.

The Shoulder Months (March – April, October – November)

Best for: A trip incorporating diverse parts of Australia.
Not as good for: The hottest areas can still be uncomfortable, especially if you're not used to the sun.

These seasons merge into each other, but as a general rule, the shoulder months provide a good time to take in all of Australia. Nowhere will be in prime season, however, these are rare months where everywhere is accessible and relatively comfortable weather wise. Just remember that the Red Center could still be touching 100°F.

Travel Costs and Organizing Your Money

Australia is not cheap. In fact, it's beginning to top the charts of expensive travel destinations. Gone are the days when a weak Australian dollar made this a backpacker's paradise. With an ever-growing mining industry, the country's economy and currency continues to accelerate and day to day expenses can make your eyes water. In addition, most visitors must consider the vast distances between destinations and the inaccessibility of some attractions. These add further pressure on the credit card. However, Australia is still achievable on most budgets as long as you're studious and selective.

Example Budgets for an Australia Trip

It's challenging to define example budgets in Australia. Much will depend on the length of your visit and how much time is spent in the cities. The following is a very rough guide and the overlap between costs is intended. Reduce it by up to 30% if you're coming for a month or more, but add 30% if the itinerary sticks to the major destinations and you're flying between everywhere. All costs are in Australian dollars. Take away 10 – 15% for costs in US dollars.

- **Super budget traveler ($70 – 90)** – With this kind of budget you'll be mostly camping (with the odd night in a dorm), cooking all your meals, carefully selecting the paid attractions, and avoiding nights out. It's certainly achievable, especially if you're renting a vehicle and making a long Australia trip.

- **Budget traveler ($90 – 120)** – This constitutes staying in hostels, cooking almost all your meals, socializing for free (not in the bars) and focusing more on natural attractions than city sights.

- **Conscientious traveler ($120 – 180)** – A decent sized budget that still means sleeping in hostels and cheap accommodation but ensures you can eat in a few restaurants, incorporate more tours and excursions, and enjoy a couple of ice cold sundowners.

- **Standard traveler - ($150 – 250)** – You're on vacation so you'll be enjoying yourself and trying not to think too much about the budget. Extra money means far more excursions and eating out, as well as not being limited to hostels and the cheapest accommodation.

- **Upmarket traveler (US$250 – 500)** – Spend more and you start living a more luxurious lifestyle, namely hanging out in bars and restaurants, taking your pick from excursions, and whizzing around the country with some more upmarket hotels.

- **Luxury traveler (US$500 +)** - Travel in style and Australia adds a coating of exclusivity to your vacation. Think boutique hotels, all the tours, plenty of time living the city life, and some of the Southern Hemisphere's finest restaurants.

Example Costs in Australia

To start building your own budget, here are some examples of typical costs. All costs are in Australian dollars.

- A good campsite - $10pp

- A dorm bed - $25 – 35pp

- A double in a dorm or budget hotel - $60 – 100

- A schooner or bottle of beer in a pub / bar - $7 – 10)

- Meal for two with drinks at a good but not gourmet restaurant - $70 - 100

- Journey of 300 miles by public transport - $20 - 40

- Full day tour of famous natural attraction – anywhere from $100 - 200

- Takeaway lunch with coffee from a cafe - $15 - 20

Easy Ways to Reduce Your Costs When Traveling in Australia

Coming from almost anywhere you will find Australia expensive. Which can be disheartening when you're on vacation and shouldn't be worrying about budgets. It's possible to swipe everything on the card and worry about it later. It's also possible to consider a few easy ways to reduce the costs and ensure that the beauty of Australia can be firmly realized.

- **Avoid peak season** – This is true everywhere in the world but magnified in a country with such high accommodation costs. Christmas and New Year prices smash through the ceiling as Australians also head out on vacation.

- **Take advantage of online accommodation offers:** There's a surplus of accommodation at off peak times and the internet is where to find the cut price deals.

- **Limit your alcohol spend** – Difficult advice, we know, but with a bottle of beer costing $8, having a few beers every evening can blow most budgets. Beer from the bottle shops is far cheaper and Australia isn't short on nice places to sit and have a drink.

- **Cook meals at municipal barbecue grounds** – Every town and destination will have at least one municipal barbecue ground, usually with a prime location overlooking the ocean. Essentially, it's a series of large gas plates that are free to use by anyone. They have a great social atmosphere with groups starting conversations with each other. Cooking your own meals reduces a large proportion of costs, and cooking at these barbecue grounds ensures you have the atmosphere of eating out.

- **Consider camping** – Few people have a positive impression of camping. Australia's campsites may have you changing your mind. Location is everything and while budget hotels are hidden down back streets, municipal campsites are normally on the beach with sweeping views. Amenities are in excellent condition and there's always a soft green patch with electricity hook up to pitch your tent.

- **Hire your own wheels:** Most of Australia's evocative outdoors is free to explore, but the cost of tours can make exploring prohibitively expensive. Even hiring a car when you're in the city means good savings on any activities outside the urban center.

- **Slow the pace:** There's so much to see that most Australia's journeys are rushed. Which doesn't suit the country's ambiance and will inevitably push the costs up. It can feel annoying to miss out but going slower is both cheaper and more enjoyable.

- **Enjoy the free stuff:** While Australia's cities are iconic destinations, the bulk of the country's appeal lies in the vast untrammeled beauty of the landscapes. National parks are cheap to enter and there's gaping expanses of primitive wilderness that are always free to explore.

Organizing Your Money

For a few years the Australian dollar was trading at a similar value to the US dollar. It's now a little weaker and you can expect to receive around 1.2 Australian for every 1 of your American. Currency exchange can be found in virtually every destination or town.

Visa and mastercard facilities are virtually universal with Australia being one of the first countries to introduce contactless payments. Likewise, almost every ATM will accept foreign cards. The main consideration when organizing money is the vast distances between destinations. Travel across the Australian outback and there might be one cash machine every 1000 miles. So stock up if you're going walkabout. Furthermore, the further you head into the desert, the less developed the communications and facilities. So carrying cash is always helpful.

Basic Travel Requirements

Australia has a very straightforward electronic visa system, or Electronic Travel Authority (ETA). This visa is electronically linked to your passport and must be applied for in advance of your arrival. Apply online at www.eta.immi.gov.au/ETA/ and it takes two to three working days. It's free for EU citizens. American and Canadian citizens will pay AUD$20. Argentinian, Brazilian and a few other eVisitor eligible countries pay a fee of UAD$130.

An ETA allows visitors to stay in Australia for up to three months. Note that a requirement of the ETA is to have a return or outbound flight. This will also be checked when you board the outbound flight.

Quarantine is strict when you land in Australia with customs officials ripping through bags to analyze mud on sneakers, tent pegs, and any fruit squashed at the bottom of a backpack. The list of prohibited substances runs to hundreds of pages but in short, don't bring any food or living matter into the country. There's a fixed AUD$200 fine for breaking the rules and a few moldy bread crusts aren't worth that kind of amount. Particular care should be taken by anyone bringing in prescribed medication. You may need to provide proof of the prescription to pass customs.

Getting to Australia

Australia is far from home. We can't be certain of where you're reading this guidebook but we're almost certain that Australia's on the other side of the world. A huge part of the travel budget is taken up by international flights. With a few competing airlines soaring across the sky, domestic air travel is relatively cheap. Therefore it's often cheapest to search for the cheapest flights to Australia, and then use domestic flights to hop to your final destination.

Sydney and Melbourne are the two largest and busiest airports. Both are situated in the southeast of Australia. Queenstown, Gold Coast, and Cairns are hubs for budget airline flights to Asia and are convenient for the East Coast (see Air Asia X and Scoot airlines). Perth is the major airport in the West. Note that it's over four hours flight to then cross Australia from Perth to Sydney.

There is no realistic land entry to Australia. A few people try, often Australians returning from Europe and trying to do it all overland. The only workable route are the container ships from Singapore to Freemantle on the West Coast.

Getting Around Australia

Moving around Australia requires a plan. Unfortunately. Distances are long, cutting through mile after mile of seemingly monotonous landscape. It's beautiful in a way, the scale of the hinterlands bringing impressions of grandeur. Yet it can be tiresome. Here are the options:

Internal Flights

In a country of this size, the mainstay of many travel itineraries are budget flights. There's an impressive network to choose from and the number of tourist focused routes has dramatically increased over the years. For example, Cairns – Ayer's Rock – Melbourne / Sydney combines the Great Barrier Reef, the big red rock, and the city. Jetstar and Tiger are the two budget airline options and are excellent for flights between the major destinations. Qantas and Virgin Australia have wide reaching networks and offer extensive choice.

Small airports are popping up on a regular basis, allowing direct access to some of Australia's famous but far-flung destinations. They're usually limited to flights to the major airports (often only Sydney and Melbourne) but are very handy. For example, with just a week in Australia you can fly Sydney to the Whitsunday Islands, then direct to Melbourne.

Hiring a Car

Hiring a vehicle is hugely popular. It's relatively cheap, offers a freedom that Australia almost demands, and ensures you can explore the vast stretches of deserted paradise the country is famous for. Competition keeps prices low, with all the major international car hire firms locking heads with locally based operators. One way travel is understandably popular and some car hire firms will wave the one way travel fee, especially if you're traveling in the opposite direction to most travelers. For example, when winter comes around most people travel north up the East Coast. Travel the other way and you can get great bargains. A second major advantage of hiring a vehicle is the excellent range of municipal campsites and cheaper accommodation in smaller towns.

Australians drive on the left and most international driving licenses are recognized. Roads are generally straight and quiet, with the greatest risk coming from falling asleep rather than hitting an obstacle. But distances are huge. Even places that look close on a map will be half a day's drive. To give you an example, travel the length of the East Coast and Melbourne to Sydney is 900kms, Sydney to Brisbane 1000kms, and Brisbane to Cairns 1700kms. Realistically, that's close to 50 hours of driving time. And the big ones: Perth to Darwin or Perth to Sydney are over 4000kms.

Hiring a Camper

Hiring a camper and traveling Australia is the kind of dream that inhabits the top of many travel bucket lists. It's surprisingly simple and the roads are awash with backpackers rumbling down the highways in their rented and often painted campers. Local companies tend to focus their efforts on different audiences and it's reasonably priced, particularly at the cramped budget end. However, if you're looking for the cheapest option, it's better to hire a car and buy camping equipment then rent a camper.

Buying a Vehicle

For trips of six weeks or more, it can be financially advantageous to purchase a vehicle and then sell it on. This is risky, because if you don't find a buyer then the vehicle lies to rot and your bank manager makes a threatening call. The six week rental price for a vehicle will roughly equate to the money you would lose when buying and then reselling the same vehicle. However, there's a few major considerations. Firstly, remember that the people who want to buy the used vehicle are people like yourself, those looking for a good deal to travel the country. So forget any notions of breaking even. Secondly, you'll probably be putting at least another 5000kms on the clock so the price of repairs can add up, as will the service to get the vehicle in decent sellable condition.

As a general rule, it's far easier to buy and sell if you travel in the opposite direction to other travelers. For example, on the East Coast, most people travel north in winter, meaning a huge surplus of vehicles without buyers in Cairns. Travel the opposite direction and you can buy cheap, then have a larger potential market to sell it on to.

Having your own vehicle means access to beaches like this one on the Great Ocean Road

Long Distance Bus Network and Hop on Hop Off Tickets

Greyhound has been crisscrossing Australia for decades and they have a huge network of domestic bus routes. While the distances are daunting, the service is excellent and the buses can be classed as luxurious; although whether they remain luxurious after 48 hours on board is a different question. The extending network of domestic flights has dramatically reduced the options for long distance road travel. Greyhound virtually runs a monopoly on routes. Ozexperience used to provide a competing hop on hop off service, but they were bought out by Greyhound in 2013.

For long single journeys between destinations, it's far more comfortable and sometimes to cheaper to fly. Greyhound offer a wide range of hop on hop off bus tickets. These are great option for single travelers and negate renting a vehicle. Tickets include flexible six month options and single route hop on hop off. Their Ozexperience brand combines the hop on hop off with tours and backpacker accommodation. This can be good value and the range of daily departures (especially on the East Coast) ensure that these tickets can offer maximum flexibility. With the variety of available ticket options, Greyhound likes to oversell what you need. It makes sense to first plan a route and then find the best value hop on hop off ticket.

Nationwide Train Network

Australian trains are not fast. They trundle across the wilderness, the remains of industrial tracks creaking beneath a couple of services per day. But these trains are beautiful. Anyone who likes train travel is likely to adore the gentle journeys through the desert and along the coast. Anyone who frowns at the thought of 24 hours on train is better off flying. Long distance Australian trains are now firmly tourist services and cost more than the equivalent flights. Great Southern Railways operates the majority of the idealized routes, with trains that connect Sydney, Melbourne, Adelaide, Alice Springs, Darwin, and Perth. Queensland Rail is an option for rail travel in the northern half of the East Coast.

Such long distances inevitably mean relatively high ticket prices. However, you're paying for the experience of crossing Australia's big red desert without having to sit behind a wheel. A couple of rail passes may be of use, including the East Coast Discovering Pass and a handful of three month explorer passes sold by Great Southern Railways.

To cross Australia and take in the scale and mystique of a whole continent consider:

- The **Indian Pacific** from Perth to Sydney, traversing Australia from west to east.

- Rumbling across the Red Center, **TheGhan** from Adelaide to Darwin.

- **The Overland** from Adelaide to Melbourne and then the 12 hour journey from Melbourne to Sydney.

Suburban City Transport

The major cities have excellent public transport networks. In particular, traveling around Melbourne on the old tram system is both efficient and an ode to yesteryear. Dependent on the city, you'll be on a mix of underground trains, trams, and local buses. There are good maps, helpful staff, and all the signs are in English. In short, if you can't decipher Australia's suburban transport networks then you're going to struggle everywhere else in the world. Bare in mind the high individual costs of single trips. For stays of two days or more in a city then it works out cheaper to buy travel passes.

Where to Stay

Australia's accommodation is very much like the country it graces. It's laid-back and expensive. Real estate prices in cities and major destinations can be extortionate, making the price for the cheapest room seem painfully high. These prices equate to good quality. Even the cheapest hotels are of a good standard and there's often little need to spend more. With a higher budget, upmarket Australian hotels compete amongst the best in the world, from unique island retreats to waterfront boutique hotels in the city. If you need to cut costs then the municipal campsites often redefine stereotypes about camping.

The Australian accommodation style is sometimes hard to define. Travel along the coast and there's hundreds of tiny destinations with locally run caravan parks and guesthouses. Arrive in the city and you could watching the sunset from the 20th floor. Plush shining hotels stand on the waterfront, but so do municipal campsites. It's not necessarily a case of something for everyone, more that there's almost always options wherever you arrive. As a general rule, the larger the city the more it's dominated by chains and international brands. Remote destinations are where you find owner managed accommodation with an invariably tranquil feel. Breakfast is usually included (except camping) and they tend to follow the colonial British style of sticking everything in the frying pan. They're filling, if not at all healthy.

The need to book in advance depends on the destination. In cities and major tourist destinations it's almost essential. During peak season there can be a dearth of hotel beds and charging around a city looking for one isn't enjoyable. Out of season, you can find some excellent deals on the major travel sites like www.booking.com and www.tripadvisor.com. But when you're out in the sticks, online reservation systems don't suit the old-world tradition. It's easy to adjust the itinerary as you go, although it's always wise to call in advance if you're arriving after sun down.

Here are the options (all prices in Australian dollars).

Camping ($10 – 20pp) – Forget any nasty preconceptions about camping. Australia's campsites usually occupy prime position in town and the amenities are among the best you'll find anywhere in the world. Most will have a barbecue area that provides a social atmosphere of sharing sundowner drinks. All campsites will have electricity hook ups which are usually an additional $5-10. It's similarly priced whether you're in a camper or pitching a tent. Camp 4 is a regularly updated book containing virtually every campsite in Australia. It's an excellent and essential resource.

Static Caravans ($20 – 30pp) – Some campsites will rent out static caravans, particularly those in remote coastal areas. It's another cheap option that offers wonderful location.

Hostels ($25 – 40pp) – Australia's hostels throb with life, hundreds of reveling backpackers turning them into debauched places of drunkenness. The vibe is usually young, party, and intense. Within a day you're likely to have two dozen new friends and a hangover. They're not always places for a good night's sleep, and if you're not in the mood to drink, it's easy to feel left out. Quality varies dramatically, from long standing hostels with swimming pools and multiple bars, to cheaply concocted wannabes. www.hostelworld.com and www.hostelbookers.com are good places for checking user reviews.

Owner managed guesthouses and accommodation ($40 – 80pp) – Fueling off the beaten track Australia is an eclectic bunch of owner managed accommodation, varying from cottages on the beach to old wooden guesthouses and roadside motels. They're run by real Aussie characters, often resembling famed stereotypes as they potter around and serve endless pots of tea. It's relatively cheap and always memorable. In rural Australia these places could be your only option.

Budget Hotels ($50 – 100pp) – Australia's budget hotels are cheap and cheerful, normally tucked away on the edges of town and fulfilling everything you would need for a decent night's sleep. Don't expect originality but it's difficult to find anything to complain about.

Mid-range hotels and guesthouses ($80 – 150pp) – There's a huge range available here, from international chains to locally managed guesthouses. Prices are dictated by location, with major destinations double the cost of elsewhere. Popular beach destinations often feature a large mid-range resort, usually affordable to all but not always winning prizes for inimitability.

Luxury hotels ($150 +) - Australia knows how to treat its visitors and the upmarket hotels can rival those found anywhere in the world. You'll pay for it, but the price tag comes with what the cheaper options don't provide; great service, a room with a view, and an idealized location.

Chapter 3
Immersing Yourself in Australia

Australians are as distinguishable as they come. Confident, sociable, always displaying a wide grin, and often keeping the mood light-hearted. They're fiercely proud of their country and aren't afraid to show it. Some mistake this pride for arrogance. While there's a certain brashness to the archetypal Aussie, they're always welcoming and immersing yourself in Australia involves accepting the invitation. Whether that's for a cold beer, a conversation, or a nod hello on the street. Australia is eminently more enjoyable when you settle into their rhythm and the following should help smooth out the transformation into the land down under.

Relax

Australia's atmosphere is one of serenity and laughter. Even Sydney has an air of tranquility when compared to large cities around the world. While it's difficult to leave the tick list at home, charging around on a mission for iconic photos doesn't suit the country's style. Relax, allow yourself to unwind, and go with the flow. Australia is one of a select few countries where everything runs on time yet there's no anal dedication to time keeping. A country where everything works but nobody sacrifices fun for functionality. It's a country where things just seem to work out as soon as you relax.

Bring a Sense of Humor

In some countries, a sense of humor is an essential antidote for things always going wrong. That's not the case in Australia. You'll need a sense of humor because without it, the Australians will delight in poking fun and making jokes at your expensive. Aussies are invariably light-hearted and if you can take a little humorous jab then you'll get on fine. Don't get offended. It's just the Australian way of making friends, even if what's said could be construed as an insult back home. And don't be afraid to throw a joke back. They'll like you more for trying it.

Be Sociable

Australia is lived outdoors and there's an endearing sociability to almost every destination. In the cities, strangers greet strangers far more than you might encounter elsewhere in the world. In rural area, strangers are a rare phenomenon for the locals, so expect a few intrigued looks and smiles hello. Australians are talkative and interesting. As you settle into the country, you'll quickly lose the social inhibitions that prevent befriending strangers back home.

Respect Aboriginal Culture

Aboriginal culture is vastly misunderstood and has been virtually stamped off this island. What's left of it remains the planet's oldest surviving culture, an ode to living harmoniously with the natural environment. In recent years, indigenous tribes have been reclaiming their land, perhaps the most impressive example being at Mossman Gorge (see Chapter 9: The East Coast). There's a certain mystique and allure but note that much of indigenous Aboriginal culture is not for visitors; e.g. ceremonies and culturally significant places. Respecting and supporting Aboriginal run tourism or activities is the best way to help preserve this ancient culture. Read more about Aboriginal culture in Chapter 10: The Red Center.

The Tourist Information Office

In remote Australia, the local pub or store also doubles as the tourist information office; sometimes in an informal way (see listen to the locals below), and sometimes in a way to cut costs. Australia hasn't been the fastest in formalizing a Tourist Information system and the availability of information depends heavily on the popularity of your destination. Government run Tourist Information Offices can be found in some destinations although they often seem underfunded and can be hidden away. For example, the Cairns boardwalk bursts with competing tour companies offering a similar selection of tours; the impartial Tourist Information Office is practically hidden. There will always be somewhere to garner up to date, detailed and localized, information. Tourist information is just one option, whether it's government run or otherwise.

Listen to the Locals

In rural areas, being social is essential for making your trip a safe and enjoyable one, especially if you have your own transport. It you're heading out to a remote destination in the desert, it's often essential to stop in the nearest town and inform the locals (usually the local pub) of where you're going. If the car breaks down you could be 200 miles from anywhere, so you'll be glad when a search party gets sent out.

Remote areas are where you'll find the closest images to the stereotype of a crocodile hunter in a corked hat pulling out a three foot knife. While they might not look like Mick Dundee, there's a good chance that people living in remote Australia have hardly ever left their surrounding region. Asking them about what to do in Sydney is pointless. But they'll know everything essential about the road ahead; how many kilometers to the next gas station, what to look out for in between, the name of the guesthouse owner in the next village, and how many hours to the next destinations along the road. It's in-depth knowledge that even the most detailed of guidebooks couldn't have and they're keen to share it. The surrounding area may seem harsh, foreign, yet endearing beautiful. To the locals it's home.

Information from your Guesthouse / Hostel / Hostel / Campsite

The tourism community in Australia is small. While the burgeoning popularity of the country may have seen the number of tour operators multiply, this is still a place where everyone knows everyone who knows everyone. So the best place for impartial localized information is usually your accommodation. They understand their clientele and which tour operators or experiences receive the best reviews. They're usually passionate about ensuring visitors enjoy themselves and are likely to be more reliable than Trip Advisor reviews. Especially in smaller destinations, the guesthouse owners know who has been around for decades and which company has just started out with a brazen marketing strategy.

It's not just tour operators. The accommodation owner is the archetypal town cryer, promoting what's great about the town on any given day. They'll tell you where to find the best fish and chips for 500 miles, which beach is home to nesting turtles, and tonight means two for one on beers at the local pub. They have the fountain of knowledge that only a local can have, a cascade of information that's regularly altered by feedback from their guests.

Staying Safe

Australia is generally a country of low crime although following the basic precautions is always wise. This is a country virtually devoid of an underclass, so the sight of down and out characters trying to pick pockets isn't common.

In rural areas, the atmosphere may feel like one of locals leaving their door unlocked, but there are sporadic reports of car break-ins or, to be more specific, tourists leaving doors unlocked and returning to find a missing radio.

While the locals don't pose much of a threat, the environment can be one of the most challenging on the planet. Sun, intense heat, and a lack of water, all add up to a disaster for anyone unprepared. It could be hundreds of miles to the next settlement so everyone must pack ample water in case of breakdown. Respecting the environment is essential to staying safe and healthy. You'll quickly learn that those wide-brimmed hats with dangling corks have a purpose.

This is also a country of renowned wild animals. Crocodiles really do live here; that wasn't just a fictional Hollywood narrative. If a river contains crocodiles there will be a sign indicating the threat. Just because you can't see them doesn't mean it's safe to have a dip; you wouldn't be the first to have a set of razored-teeth around your ankles. Murky rivers aren't that enticing, but sapphire ocean waters are what vacations are all about. Unfortunately, Northern Australia is home to salt water crocodiles, the predators especially common around Darwin. Everyone and everything will inform you of the risk. But every now and then there's a tourist that risks it and doesn't come back.

When driving, also keep a watch out for kangaroos and crossing wildlife. This is particularly problematic at night, where unlit highways become scenes of hefty collisions. On a long road trip you're likely to spot a roadkill every couple of hundred miles. A cargo truck versus a kangaroo isn't much of a contest. A rental vehicle or campervan colliding with a kangaroo will leave both parties in irreparable states of damage.

Think poisonous spiders or biting snakes and the Australian outback is one of the first places that springs to mind. In reality, locals can go a lifetime without seeing them and incidents are extremely rare. Still, if you're going walkabout in the bush, always wear closed footwear.

Staying Healthy

Staying healthy is also defined by the intensity of the environment. If relentless sun and heat wasn't enough, there's a large hole in the ozone layer directly above Australia. The country has the highest incidence of skin cancer anywhere in the world, and that's with a very conscious and respectful population. Australia is not a country for tanning oil and baking on the beach in the midday sun. It's a place for factor 30 suncream, staying hydrated, and covering up when necessary.

Healthcare and hospital facilities are amongst the very best in the world and you'll be in fine hands in case of emergency. For many decades, outback Australia has been connected by a flying doctor service, so although you may be a few hundred miles from a hospital, there will always be a way to get you there quickly. Be certain to bring copies of your travel insurance documentation. Medical bills in Australia could make you bankrupt if you have to foot the bill.

There is no disease or major health threat other than what is found in Europe of the US. No additional immunizations are required.

Working Holidays in Australia

Working in Australia is one of the world's most renowned backpacker travel dreams. For anyone under 30 with a Western passport, obtaining a one year work visa is relatively straightforward. Work is also fairly easy to find, as long as you don't mind getting your knees dirty. Australia relies on a large immigrant population to fill the jobs that the locals aren't interested in; namely waiting tables and picking fruit. The pay can be exceptional when compared to the rest of the world and a three month fruit picking job can save the cash for three months of traveling. You'll need to arrive in season (either for tourists or ripening fruit) to get the job, with far more choice offered in far-flung unheard of destinations. There's usually an eclectic bunch of international young people to hang out (and get drunk) with, but it's no picnic. These jobs are tiring.

After 12 months, you can apply for a second year working visa. The pre-requisite being working for three months in the agricultural industry (i.e. fruit picking), and having your work signed off by a registered employer. Staying any longer than two years is tricky. You'll need to be sponsored by an employer or be experienced in a trade that's on Australia's wanted list.

Chapter 4
An Overview of the Destination Chapters

This guidebook has divided Australia into clear geographical chunks or regions. These don't always correlate to administrative boundaries but provide the clearest way to present Australia from a visitor's perspective. Each destination chapter provides an introduction, a section on travel essentials, and then detailed information on the travel experiences to find. These are presented in geographical order, enabling you to clearly map out a route. Links between regions are also provided.

With this approach, each region has an established aerial entry point that is also the crossroads for transport heading out in multiple directions. Here's an overview:

Chapter 5: Sydney and Around: Iconic Sydney dazzles from all angles and finds itself at the centerpiece of most itineraries, not least because it's home to the country's busiest airport. This is one of the world's most pristine and memorable cities, and that's before you consider the picturesque scenery shimmering in the periphery. This chapter covers the city and everything within easy day trip reach.

Chapter 6: Melbourne and Victoria: Heading south from Sydney it's 900kms to Melbourne and the state of Victoria. Artistic and alternative, the area provides a funky paradigm not seen elsewhere. It's still undeniably Australian, especially when the beaches bake in summer.

Chapter 7: South Australia: Keep following the coastline, along the Great Ocean Road to Adelaide, the major entry point of the South Coast. Come here for rolling vineyards, beautifully remote beaches, and laid-back Australia at its finest.

Chapter 8: Tasmania: The island of Tasmania is vastly different from the mainland; rugged, green, and handcrafted for exploring the great outdoors. It's cast adrift just south of Melbourne.

Chapter 9: The East Coast: From Sydney a single highway runs 2700kms up the East Coast to Cairns. This is Australia's most popular overland route, a concoction of beach, outback Australia, rainforest, tropical reef, and cute towns. Not everybody does the full distance and this chapter is split into two; Sydney to Gold Coast and then then Brisbane to Cairns. Both Brisbane and Gold Coast have major international airports.

Chapter 10: The Red Center: Australia's scorched red desert provides the backdrop of dreams. It's vast, desolate, and exceeding all preconceived reverie about the country. This is a massive geographical area that's crossed by virtually only one road, the Stuart Highway, and this provides the basis of the chapter.

Chapter 11: The West Coast: Less visited than the East yet equally hypnotic, the West Coast is about a stunningly remote coastline, one that's patrolled by whale sharks and virtually devoid of footprints. Some visitors prefer it because it's less touristy than the East. Other visitors prefer the action and greater concentration of destinations on the East. Undoubtedly, both are very different destinations. Perth is the major city and international entry point.

Chapter 5
Sydney and Around

Fringed by ocean rollers and green hills, and dominated by a meandering blue river, Sydney benefits from the most endearing of natural settings. This is a city harmoniously blended into its surroundings, the shimmering cityscape juxtaposed with kaleidoscopic colors. These surroundings are an effervescent highlight, from famous surfing beaches to mountains shrouded in blue haze. Head into the city's heart and the iconicity keeps coming, Sydney Opera House and Sydney Harbor Bridge as famous a city backdrop as anywhere else in the world. The center is a mix of old and new, the remaining relics of yesteryear merging with the confident exterior of modern Australia.

Despite its fame, Sydney is a relatively compact and easy to explore city. It's size is nothing on the scale of major European cities and the range of public transport is excellent.

Travel Essentials for Sydney and Around

Getting Here: Sydney is where you'll find the country's largest international airport. There are internal flights to Sydney from virtually every small airport in the country and it's the easiest destination to fit onto a travel itinerary. The airport is just outside the city center and regular trains take just 15 minutes to reach stations in the center. Sydney is also a major transport crossroads for both rail and road.

Getting Around: Sydney's local transport is excellent. Public ferries ply the Parramatta River and are both commuter transport and cheap sightseeing tour. The underground trains are also an excellent and cheap way of getting around. In the city center, distances are short and traveling on foot is both easy and enjoyable. Even the journey from Darling Harbour to Bondi Beach can be walked in an hour.

Planning an Itinerary: With the breadth of experiences on offer, Sydney normally takes up a few days in any itinerary. It's rare that you'll need more than a public transport map to connect the dots. Experiences and destinations around Sydney can all be seen on a day trip or tour, with many tour operators competing for business. From Sydney there are three major options. Going overland you can head north along the East Coast (Chapter 9) or south to Melbourne and Victoria (Chapter 6). Or you can fly out of Sydney to virtually anywhere in Australia with an airport.

Accommodation in Sydney and Around: Accommodation in Sydney is expensive and not always great value. Real estate prices are so high in Sydney that rent is quoted per week, rather than per month. So don't expect spacious rooms even in the high-end hotels. You'll find all the major international hotel chains in Sydney, each of them seeking for the prime spot above the river. Staying a little out of the Circular Quays / Darling Harbour area will bring the prices down significantly, and you'll also find many appealing options dotting the beaches.

Sydney City

Sydney Harbour Bridge

The city of Sydney is easy to explore. The Parramatta River cuts everything in two, the beaches lie to the East, and it's far more compact than people imagine for a city of such fame. Certainly confident, and at times brazen, Sydney is a rapidly developing modern city with a thousand outlets for every credit card. You'll find surf, pubs, museums, monuments, nightclubs, and a city that doesn't necessarily sleep.

- **Sydney Harbour** is the traditional center of the city, standing on the Parramatta River and framed by two world famous landmarks. The gleaming white sails of the **Sydney Opera House** are here, along with an eclectic range of bars and waterfront restaurants. One hour Opera House tours are expensive and the building's beauty is more exterior than interior. To really soak it up, consider actually getting tickets for a performance. **Circular Quays** is a major Sydney transport hub here (both subway and river). There's a huge assortment of places to eat and drink although they're on the pricey side.

- Opposite Sydney Opera House, and the perfect place for photos of the sails,is**The Rocks**, Australia's oldest settlement. It's a collection of narrow streets, the odd colonial relic, funky bars, and fine dining restaurants. The lack of traffic makes it a delightful place to wander.

- **Sydney Harbour Bridge** is the other famous landmark here, the exposed steel archway proudly marking the centerpiece of the city. Slowly walk up the steps to the peak of the bridge with the **Sydney Harbour Bridge Climb** for perhaps Australia's finest panorama; the river below, Circular Quays skyscrapers to the right, and the whole city rolling into the distance. Allow three hours for the trip.

- Follow the river beneath the Bridge and you reach **Darling Harbour.** This was the city's working class port, it's now Sydney's most exclusive and tourist grabbing neighborhood, glistening above the river and home to a boisterous collection of high-rising international hotels. You'll find **Sydney Aquarium**, cinemas, restaurants, old war ships, and cocktail bars.

- **Sydney River Cruises** depart from both Darling Harbour and Circular Quays. Essentially, they offer a boat tour of the city, heading down and then back up the river with iconic views throughout and a commentary coming through the P.A system. There's an array of options; lunch cruises, dinner cruises, nighttime cruises, and cruises laughing all the way to the bank. A cheaper alternative of the same thing are the public **Sydney Ferries** that tour the river. For less than $10 you can get the same cruise, just without the commentary. The most memorable section is from Darling Harbour to Circular Quays, as it passes beneath the Bridge before running alongside the Opera House.

- The river isn't the only unique way to explore Sydney. **Cycle and segway tours** are increasingly popular, providing an overarching overview of the city's core sights in just a couple of hours. **Helicoptertours** are a more expensive option, but such iconic aerial views can't be found in many places in the world.

- **Oxford Street** is the alternative side to Sydney; colorful, gay friendly, always fun, and more dive bar than champagne bar. It's a place of debauched nightclubs and there's a seedy air after dark, which makes it even more fun.

- It's merely a 20 minute walk between Darling Harbour and Circular Quays across the heart of the city. Sydney's few remaining old buildings are seen here, including the wonderfully opulent Queen Victoria Building and the excellent boutique **shopping around George and Pitt Streets**. With shops and restaurants galore, it's a place for exploring at will and **getting lost down side streets**. One of the finest old buildings is the **Art Gallery of New South Wales,** complete with wonderful portrayals of Aboriginal art.

- Cross Sydney Harbour Bridge and the city begins to spread. There's plenty to find here. **Sydney Fish Market** is smelly and atmospheric, a place for negotiating a kilo of fresh catch and getting it delivered straight from the barbecue. Head out further into the suburbs and you reach **Sydney's Olympic Stadium**, explorable via stadium tours but best experienced when there's an international rugby match being played (see the box below on sport in Australia). **Milson Point** provides stunning views across the river to the Opera House and the **Olympic Pool** is perfectly situated for a swim and a chance to soak it all up.

- Sydney exudes a youthful exuberant ambiance, epitomized by the suburbs that line the ocean rollers. **Bondi Beach** is the most famous, a narrow bay dominated by hundreds of surfers. **Surf schools** give lessons here, although the crowded waters aren't always conducive to learning. **The Bondi to Coogee Coastal Walkway** connects the beach suburbs on this side of the river - **Cloverly, Bronte, Coogee, Tamarama**, and Bondi - each surf destinations and cute beachside neighborhoods in their own right. Bondi is easily the most crowded.

Come in the evening and you'll find the walkway patrolled by active locals out jogging. Come at any time of day and it's a wonderfully easy walk.

- Keep going south and the beaches become less crowded, each overlooked by towering headlands and excellent restaurants. These **Southern Beaches** are where the locals hang out, with **Cronulla** being the pick of the bunch. Start here and a walkway connects other quiet strips of sand.

- On the opposite side of the river, **Manly** is one of the quaintest neighborhoods, a serene place of surf, cafes, and easygoing beach life. For long stays in Sydney, staying here is a cheaper and more tranquil option. **Manly Beach** provides a longer and less crowded beach for a day of tanning, and taking the **Manly Ferry** is easily as charming as any Sydney Harbour Cruise. **The Spit Bridge to Manly Coastal Walk** winds up and down dramatic cliffs, with sailing boats and sheltered bays omnipresent throughout.

Around Sydney

Leave the cityscape behind and the landscape is dominated by green hills and valleys, the roads quickly winding into rural areas and fresh air. For visitors on a tight time schedule, these surrounding areas provide an easy glimpse at the beauty of untamed Australian landscape. Those with more time can easily spend the best part of a week weaving between these destinations. All the following can be accessed by self driving or on tours from Sydney.

- A shimmering blue haze floats across the green eucalyptus clad valley of the **Blue Mountains**, this UNESCO World Heritage Site the most popular day trip from Sydney. Multiple **lookout points** gaze across the juxtaposition of sandstone pinnacles and forested undergrowth. Short **hiking trails** take you into indigenous rainforest with the **world's steepest train track** taking you back uphill. There's also a **cable car** traversing the valley, although it's only worth it in good weather. It's a huge area to explore and an immersion in wild Australia very close to the city.

The Three Sisters in the Blue Mountains

- Only a little further afield, the warm climate of the **Hunter Valley** make it a world famous wine growing region. There's vineyards galore, rows of grapes dominated by green mountains and sweeping views. Many Australian wine exporters come from here and they're joined by more boutique cellars. Almost all offer wine tasting, but be aware of Australia's very strict drink driving laws. Numerous Hunter Valley Wine Tours run from Sydney and ask around for a company suiting your style. Some are tailored for young people wanting to party, others for more serious connoisseurs.

- Sydney's waters hold treasures although they're often oversold and over-marketed. **Whale tours** offer inconsistent chances to spot the great mammals and decent **scuba diving** can be found just off shore. Both are options if Sydney is your only destination. If you're heading to either East or West Coast it's better to save it for later.

- Just south of the city, the **Southern Highlands** are a less crowded and less touristic alternative to the Blue Mountains. A place of hiking trails, picnic spots, and escaping the city.

Sport in Australia

Australians are proudly crazy about sport, especially when it comes to supporting their country. If Australia is playing cricket or rugby then the whole country stops and watches. National league sport is also hugely popular and not just for what happens on the pitch. It's usually a prime excuse to enjoy a few beers, have a good shout, and chat to the person sat next to you; very much iconically Australian. At the weekends in any city there's likely to be a live match being played. Stadiums are large and impressive, and the atmosphere is always one of friendly fun. But you're not watching soccer. Australians play a different kind of sport:

- **Cricket** is a complicated sport, even to the experienced. It's essentially a team sport with a bat and a ball; you could compare it to baseball but that's grossly simplistic. Some matches last three hours, others last for five days. But fear not. You don't get bored as the crowd uses the game as an excuse for getting drunk all day.

- **Rugby league** is the country's most popular sport and there's only been three occasions when the green and golds *weren't* world champions. It could be compared to American football, except players tackle each other without padding or helmets and the game isn't stopped after every tackle.

- **Rugby union** is kind of the same as rugby league, just with 15 players a side instead of 13. It's less popular but look out for the Super Rugby championship from March to September, when the best few teams from Australia, New Zealand, and South Africa compete.

- **Australian Rules Football** or Aussie Rules, is another baffling sport. Fast, combative, and played on 120 meter long circular pitch, it's as unique as the country that invented it. It's very popular in Melbourne and Victoria.

Chapter 6
Melbourne and Victoria

For some 200 years, Sydneyers and Melbourners have been arguing about whose city rules. Melbourne revels in offering something alternative; the streets a mishmash of old-world charm and modern shopping boutiques, the riverside alive with the tunes of buskers, and surrounding Victoria sprawling around green forests and empty beaches. Tucked onto the southeastern tip of Australia, Melbourne and Victoria are decidedly balmy in summer, although the winter rain doesn't quite reflect the weather stereotypes of the country.

Melbourne is Australia's biggest city and it's the capital of the country's second smallest state, Victoria.

Travel Essentials for Melbourne and Victoria

Getting Here: Melbourne International Airport is the second busiest in the country and flights arrive here from around the world. Like Sydney, Melbourne is a major domestic hub and it's easy to fly direct here from most of the country's smaller domestic airports. The airport is around 45 minutes drive outside the city center and there are buses from the airport. Coming by road, Melbourne is 10 – 12 hours from Sydney (see the box below), or 12 – 14 hours from Adelaide (see chapter 7).

Getting Around: Melbourne trams have been rumbling around for the best part of 70 years and they're an iconic choice for suburban transport. Outside the center, a developed underground and overground train network goes just about everywhere.

Planning an Itinerary: Melbourne tends to be visited at the start or end of a trip. It's the southern end of the East Coast and a major aerial transport hub. During summer, a sublime overland trip is to head west along the South Coast, driving along the Great Ocean Road and continuing to Southern Australia and Adelaide (See Chapter 7). Melbourne invariably woos its visitors and many regret not having enough time to soak up the atmosphere.

Accommodation in Melbourne and Victoria: Melbourne sprawls, extending over a huge area. City center hotels tend to be of the high rising high priced kind, but the outer lying suburbs and beaches offer more charming alternatives.

Melbourne

Melbourne delights in its artistic twang, the streets ever-cultural and looking to provide something unique. Colonial remains stand between modern skyscrapers, arcades spill out onto narrow Chinese markets, a hundred nationalities mingle on the streets, but then it's not far before the waters of the Southern Ocean roll before your eyes. Like Sydney, a river cuts the city in two (the Yarra), and a series of beaches form the centerpiece of the suburbs. A further similarity is found in the compact nature of the city center. Unlike its northern rival, Melbourne spreads over a huge area, the collection of beaches indelibly quiet and rolling beneath scorching all day sunshine in summer.

- The **Melbourne riverside** epitomizes the fun easygoing nature of a city, buskers providing the soundtrack and skyscraper lights reflecting in the water. It's a great place to wander in the evenings, the line of cocktail bars and restaurants almost impossible to ignore. On one side of the river is the city's historical heartbeat, while to the south lies the **Southbank**, a hub for partying, the arts, and some fine restaurants.

The Melbourne Riverside

- The city's **original architecture** has managed to survive the bulldozer better than elsewhere in Australia. These buildings form an ode to yesteryear, a time of engineering indulgence and Victorian style, and their juxtaposition with modern Melbourne is at times bizarre. Arguably most impressive is the 19th century **Royal Arcade** and **Flinders Street Station,** but also check out the buildings along **Clarendon Street towards Port Melbourne**. There's also the **Shrine of Remembrance, St Patrick's Cathedral, St Paul's Cathedral,** and the **Royal Exhibition Building**

- Melbourne rewards those who give it time. Each district has its distinct flavor and an afternoon in each provides an immersion in the city's originality. **Richmond and Collingwood** have an old-school European working class feel, full of atmospheric pubs for a leisurely late afternoon.

- Melbourne is a **shopper's city**, the arcades combining boutique elegance with popular high-street brands. The locals pride themselves on looking different and the compact city center is easy to explore on foot. In particular, ambient **Delgraves Street** and the elegant **Block Arcade** are worth exploring even if you hate shopping. Further afield, for high-end and boutique shopping, check out the suburbs of **Toorak, Prahran, and South Yarra.**

- Smoke rises and smells raft across the Southern hemisphere's largest open-air market, **Queen Victoria Market**. It's a place for food lovers, the eclectic selection of food impressing every palate. There's a sprinkling of shops and always a fun atmosphere.

- **Melbourne's nightlife** is more underground and alternative than Sydney, with less tourist centered bars and more live music.

- Melbourne and Victoria is the home of **Australian Rules Football**, the endemic sport that appears confusing to almost every visitor. It's 18 men on each side, played with an oval ball on a circular field that's 120 meters across. It's fast, aggressive, and good fun. The locals are crazy about it and crowds of 50,000+ watch it live at the **Melbourne Cricket Ground**. You can get tickets at the stadium as the famous ground holds over 80,000. Outside match days, Australia's oldest and largest stadium is worth exploring on a stadium tour. Inside the stadium you'll find the **National Sports Museum**.

- Melbourne enjoys its status as **Australia's cultural hub**, the galleries and museums reflecting a commitment to ingenuity and promoting the country's famous and underground talent. There's a hub of activity at the **Arts Centre Melbourne**. Also check out the **Melbourne Museum**, the **State Library of Victoria**, and the interactive **Australian Centre for the Moving Image.** For an alternative look at local culture, wander down **Hosier Lane** and admire the vibrant graffiti.

- Deserving of its own entry, the **National Gallery of Victoria** is Australia's oldest and easily its most impressive. With a range of exhibitions covering the old and the new it can excite just about everyone.

- **Melbourne's beaches** might not be all year round paradise but they're delightfully chilled on the sand while buzzing on the beachside. The beaches around **St Kilda** are the main choice close to the city center, and it's where you'll find some good value hostels. Expect tanning during the day, gay friendly partying in the evening, and somewhere open till 4am every night of the week.

- Head further south from St Kilda and the **southeastern suburbs** provide an ongoing **collection of beaches** that stretch all the way to the very south of Australia. With excellent suburban train connections, these can both be day trips or a serene base if you're staying for a week or more. **Frankston** and **Mornington** are increasingly popular bases.

Victoria

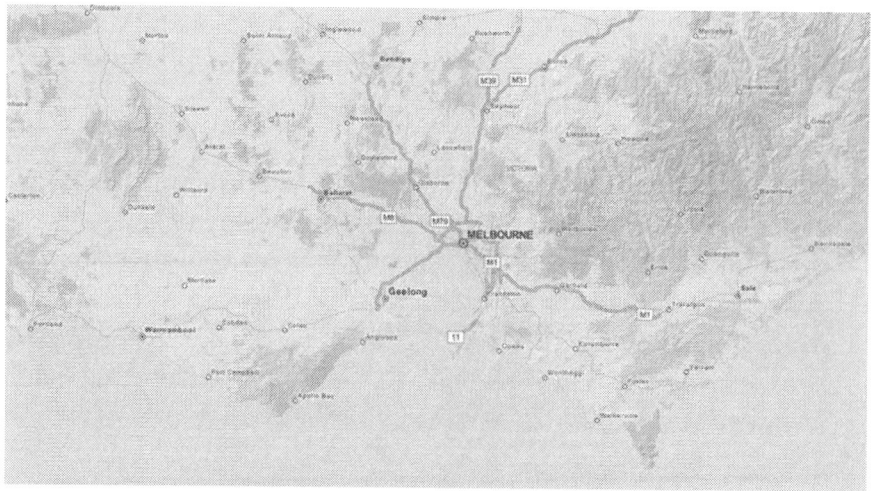

©Openstreetmap Contributors

The surrounding state of Victoria is as unique as Melbourne and it's most commonly explored as day trips from the city. With more time, many of these attractions can easily take up a few days of your time. They're inevitably fair-weather destinations, scorching and splendid in summer but often windy and wet during the winter months.

Note that most attractions and experiences lie along the coast. When planning an overland journey into South Australia and Adelaide, the road passes through many of these, including the famous Great Ocean Road.

- Victoria is the last remaining **Australian haven of the koala**, the eucalyptus forests where you'll see them sleeping on branches. The bashful creatures are not always easy to find, often hiding tucked away and hiding. Echidna Walkabout offer an excellent koalas and kangaroos in the wild tour, with a tracker going ahead and providing GPS points so you can't miss them. Under your own steam, all the destinations below are a great chance to see koalas, kangaroos, and even emus (just keep your eyes peeled).

- Just northeast of Melbourne the valleys undulate and the green hills being to rise above the city. The **Yarra Ranges National Park** offer easy day hiking and mountain bike trails within an hour of the city center, but slightly further afield, the slopes begin to burst with ripening grapes. **The Yarra Valley** is a wine connoisseurs destination, home to what's widely regarded as amongst the world's finest chardonnays. Large export vineyards and smaller cellars can be toured, with the valley's best produce being of the white variety. Tours can be easily arranged in Melbourne.

- From St Kilda and the Southeastern suburbs the road winds down to the **Southern tip of mainland Australia**. Windswept and wild, the **Wilsons Promontory National Park** is a desolate stretch of beach and dolphins swimming just off shore. There's a couple of spots for hiking but the main attraction is gazing out from the end of Australia, next stop Antarctica. It's hard to reach without your own transport. If you have got wheels, there's an easy stop on route at **Agnes Falls**.

- Due west the inland road towards South Australia gets few visitors, most taking the Great Ocean Road. The region's gold mining history can be discovered in **Ballarat** and around 250kms from Melbourne, the mountains of **Grampians National Park** rise spectacular from the plains. It's a hiker's paradise, but the scenic drive from **Halls Gap to Dunkeld** is also recommended. Over half of Victoria's Aboriginal art can be found in the caves and rocks, here, and there's impressive views all around. The visitor's center at Halls Gap and the **Brambuk National Park and Cultural Centre** can provide detailed information.

- Travel southwest from Melbourne and the beaches come at increasing frequency. **Geelong** has practically been subsumed into Melbourne but retains its own working class beachfront character. Continue for another 30 minutes and the beaches of **Torquay and Anglesea** lie beneath towering cliffs. They're ideal for surfers and sun tanners alike, and mark the start of the Great Ocean Road.

- World renowned and the number one day trip from Melbourne, the **Great Ocean Road** is a dramatic cliff clinging highway that weaves along the Southern Ocean and cuts through large swathes of native forest and farmland. It's undoubtedly a beautiful drive, with dozens of beaches to stop at and hundreds of potential photo opportunities. Walkways head into indigenous forest and then the road rolls through steeply undulating farmland. The highlights are the **12 Apostles and London Bridge**, rocky pinnacles cast adrift from the cliffs and standing isolated in the water like giant's fingers. **Cliffside walkways** take you parallel to them while **helicopter rides** soar above them. Note that seeing the Great Ocean Road is at least a 12 hour return trip from

Melbourne. Splitting up the journey is more enjoyable and this road also forms the start of the overland trip to Adelaide.

London Bridge on the Great Ocean Road

Notes on the Overland Journey Between Sydney and Melbourne

Any guesses for the capital of Australia? It's Canberra. *"Canberwhat?"* you may ask. As both cities vied for supremacy, they refused to backdown in a determined battle to become capital. A compromise was found in building Canberra, equidistant between the two and about as soulless as city as you can find in the Southern Hemisphere. Unless you're into ticking off capital cities, there's not much point in visiting. However, the overland journey between Sydney and Melbourne presents two evocative options:

- A shorter inland route cuts through Canberra and skirts alongside the Snowy Mountains, the roof of Australia that becomes white in winter. Sealed roads provide dramatic mountain views, with the **Alpine Way** and **Snowy Mountains Highway** easy detours through white and green. You'll also find skiing here. It's not the Alps or Rocky Mountains but it's a good day out and easy to arrange from Canberra.

- A longer coastal route traverses uninhabited sand and a series of rarely connected beachside towns. With towering cliffs, ocean-weathered bays, and crashing surf, this coastal route is an easy glimpse at Australia's coastline without committing to endless hours of travel time (it's merely 1100kms).

Chapter 7: South Australia

Endless miles of beaches without footprints, evocative stretches of arid red hinterland, islands covered in hopping marsupials, famous wine valleys, Aboriginal culture...South Australia seems to feature everything on a visitor's tick list. However, it's the least visited of the Australian destinations. Covering a vast almost deserted section of the central south, the region's remoteness and lack of iconic sights see it slip under most tourist radars. That helps make South Australia arguably the country's most laid-back destination, a place where nobody takes life too seriously and there's always time for another cold beer. Journeys here are limited by the few roads there are, the adventures tending to be either coastal or straight north to the Red Center (see Chapter 10).

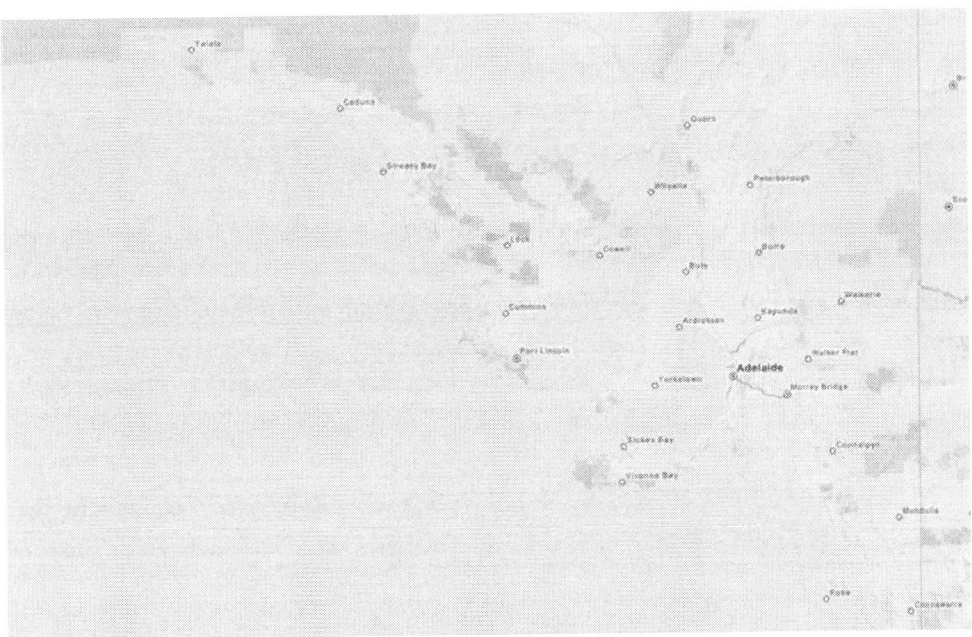

©Openstreetmap Contributors

Travel Essentials for South Australia

Getting Here: Adelaide has an international airport and is the aerial entry point. Domestic flights land here from all over the country. Adelaide is also a hub for all the long distance Great Southern Railway routes, and has direct services to Sydney, Perth, and Darwin. Coming by land, it's 12 hours from Melbourne via the Great Ocean Road, about 18 hours from Sydney, three long days from Perth, and four days to Darwin.

Getting Around: While public transport can take you all across this region, services are sporadic and you may have to stick around for a couple of days before moving on. Note that distances are large and you'll need time to explore anything further than Adelaide and its surrounding attractions.

Planning an Itinerary: If you've reached Adelaide overland, then there's a good chance you're on a long journey. Adelaide is the crossroads, now it's a question of going east, north, or south. Those flying in to Adelaide can choose to explore the surrounding attractions or use the city as the start of a long overland journey.

Accommodation in South Australia: Usually better value and more low-key than elsewhere, with many of the smaller towns home to boutique guesthouses that bring shocks of yesteryear. The wine regions have some stunning spa retreats and elegant estates.

Adelaide and Its Surrounding Attractions

Sunny, relaxed, and spacious, Adelaide can sometimes feel like a dream retirement village. What it lacks in excitement it delivers in sheer natural beauty and elegance. While young people often give it a miss, everyone else wonders why their hometown can't be as easygoing. It's fringed by beaches and vineyards, and stuffed with organic gourmet restaurants and leisurely streets. All of the following are within day trip reach of Adelaide.

- **Adelaide** itself is a quaint base for the exploration, the cute little trams taking visitors around the city with nonchalant ease.

  - The attractions seem to cement the city's serene style; the green oasis of the **Adelaide Botanic Garden**, old portraits and classics in the **Art Gallery of South Australia**, and fragrant stores in historic **Adelaide Central Market**. Changing the pace and throwing beams of neon light into the air, **Adelaide Festival Centre** is the local attempt at being hip and not quite catching the mood.

  - The bulk of Adelaide's history lies along **North Terrace**, a mile long street of colonial buildings, cute cafes, and shops selling everything from boutique chocolate to walking sticks. Walking through the old Adelaide Arcade, also known as **Rundle Mall**, is equally charming. To go back further in time, the **South Australian Museum** offers a poignant and detailed look at Aboriginal heritage and the forefathers of the land.

- o Museums in Adelaide are some of the better ones in the country and they pick up a varied narrative of local and national history. **The Migration Museum** looks at the life of early settlers, **South Australian Maritime Museum** and **Classic Jets Fighter Museum** presents exactly what you might expect, and the **National Railway Museum** features many 19th and early 20th century trains.

- o South Australia is beaches galore, most of them bordered by yellow cliffs and gazing out onto a surfer's ocean breaks. You don't need to leave Adelaide to experience them. **Glenelg** is the most popular (although you couldn't call it crowded), **Aldinga Beach** is idyllic for long beach strolls, and **Henley Beach** is the in the know locals destination. **Maslin Beach** is widely regarded as the country's best nudist beach.

- o Jutting out across the water west of Adelaide, the **Fleurieu Peninsula** feels even more like a sun-seeker's retirement destination, a series of coastal villages providing indelibly tranquil escapes.

- o You won't find a pumping night out in Adelaide but you will find great local restaurants and a few indulgent delights. A number of tour companies offer food centered tours, and an unmissable sight is the **Haigh's Chocolates Visitor Centre**.

- 45 minutes boat ride away, **Kangaroo Island** lives up to its name. The marsupials are everywhere and not just the boxing kind. The island is the last stronghold of eucalyptus chomping koalas, and you'll struggle to go a day without seeing them. Wallabies, platypus, and echidnas are also more common than almost anywhere else in Australia. The island is a natural playground and wildlife is the core attraction. After dark, **penguins can be spotted in Kingscote and Penneshaw**. Then there are **sea lions on the beach at Seal Bay Conservation Park** and **fur seals to see in Flinders Chase National Park**. Ferries to Kangaroo

Island leave from Cape Jervis with bus connections from Adelaide provided. Upon arrival in Penneshaw, the Gateway Visitor Information Centre provides detailed information on parks, wildlife, tours, and accommodation. There's usually two main options: either hire a car and explore the island (it's impossible to get lost), or book a tour that does the same.

- World renowned **Barossa Valley** is often the main reason many people visit South Australia. A myriad of enchanting **vineyards** stretch across green plantations and meandering mountain roads. This is the Australian wine destination for the connoisseurs, home to a myriad of full-bodied and powerful grapes. There are some serious international exporters to check out here, like Wolf Blass and Penfolds. Barossa is also one of the **oldest shiraz growing regions in the world** and there's plenty of small cellars that have been keeping it local for 150 years. Barossa Valley tours are easily arranged in Adelaide. To really explore, consider staying at one of the wine estates in the valley.

- Drive south of Adelaide and the landscapes of **Mclaren Vale** immediately signal wineries, organic restaurants, and antique art stores. While not as famous as Barossa, the **vineyards** still present a sensual journey through Australian grapes. Tasting is free if you buy and tours can be arranged from Adelaide. Anyone with their own transport can connect a number of artistic dots, with **boutique and historic galleries** galore in the old colonial settlements. Pack a couple of camping chairs because there are some wonderful viewpoints over Adelaide that make for gentle sundowners.

- **Clare Valley** is the least known of South Australia's wine regions but it's not without its charm and there's a difference on the palate between the powerful flavors of Barossa and the more delicate nuances of Clare Valley. Tours arranged in Adelaide.

Remote South Australia

South Australia fulfills all dreams of outback Australia; wild white sand beaches, red desert, scorched hinterlands, journeys of ongoing beauty yet no defining highlight. These parts of the region provide evocative immersion in the remote and rural, although you should be prepared for long days on the train, behind the wheel, or gazing through the bus window. Each of the following sections provides a connection with another Australian region. Note that off the main highway, roads are unlikely to be sealed. In many cases it's not a case of planning where to stop, but stopping wherever you feel like stopping.

Between Adelaide and Melbourne / Victoria

- The road from Adelaide to Melbourne is a classic overland route, traversing the **green meets yellow landscapes of South Australia** before connecting with the Great Ocean Road in Victoria (see Chapter 6). Most popular is to drive straight down to Mount Gambier near the state boundary, before continuing into Victoria and hitting the coast at Portland. At Mount Gambier, detour slightly to gaze upon the glistening **Blue Lake**.

- Those that are more adventurous can take the coastal road south from Adelaide, and hug the ocean views. While it's not as remote as the western side of South Australia, this is an endearingly splendid journey past tiny fishing villages, beach after beach, and a **Great Ocean Road style scenery** without the bus loads of tourists. This road then meets Portland in Victoria and note that some parts are unsealed.

- Trains and buses ply an inland route, taking the more direct line between the cities.

Between Adelaide and the West Coast

- The southern coastline between Adelaide and the West Coast is one of Australia's most challenging yet picturesque drives, the various peninsulas home to the remains of mining industry and the vast extends of beaches that rarely ever get visitors. Leaving Adelaide you head into the **Yorke Peninsula**, an agricultural landscape dotted with cute seaside towns and the remains of the copper industry. Along the coast it's a place for diving and fishing adventures, as well as the trails to be found in Innes National Park. York Peninsula coaches are a good option for those on public transport.

- Leaving the Yorke Peninsula and joining the **Eyre Peninsula**, the landscape gradually becomes more arid and there's a few thousand miles of virtually deserted coastline. As the burning red of the hinterland meets the gentle sapphire of the ocean, this is a journey of lingering impressions of the planet's seductive power. But it's a long long way, with hardly a town in between. Kangaroos hop around, national parks are vast, and an intrepid spirit is rewarded when you do eventually rumble into the next destination. **Cage dive with great white sharks at Port Lincoln, swim with sea lions at Baird Bay**, and then cross the seemingly endless **Nullarbor Plain**.

- Remember, it's **four days of long driving to reach Perth on the West Coast**. So even after you've cleared the Eyre Peninsula and hit Western Australia, there's still a long remote journey to do (see Chapter 11: The West Coast).

- The train from Adelaide to Perth cuts directly through the iconic scenery. Going by bus, it's more enjoyable to break the journey up at destinations in the Yorke and Eyre peninsulas.

Between Adelaide and the Red Center

Adelaide marks the start of the Stuart Highway, named after the first explorer to chart a route south to north through the heart of Australia. Running past Uluru and Alice Springs all the way to Darwin in the north (see Chapter 10), this is probably Australia's most deserted and iconic roads. At a bare minimum, allow four days of driving through nothingness. And remember this is desert, as raw and inhospitable as it can be, so stock up well if you're driving.

- Trains and buses take the same route as cars as it's practically the only route through the heart of Australia. With so few places on route, almost everyone making this journey will stop in the same places.

- Leaving Adelaide, the road passes through Port Augusta, the jumping off point for the Flinders Ranges, and Mount Remarkable National Park. Both present some stunning options for hiking, the natural amphitheaters a place to explore and get lost. Port Augusta is the last decent sized settlement for an awful long way. You cut through the often parched landscapes of Lake Torrens and Lake Gairdner national parks before hitting raw Australian outback. Watch out for the kangaroos as you journey into the Red Center with Alice Springs or Uluru the likely next stop (see Chapter 10).

Chapter 8: Tasmania

Wonderfully rugged and indelibly wild, the island of Tasmania is very different from the rest of Australia. It's topography and atmosphere is more reminiscent of neighboring New Zealand than mainland Australia, with almost half the island designated as protected national park. Green mountains, gaping lakes, thick forests, hidden beaches...Tasmania is an outdoor lovers paradise, lauded by hikers and explorers from all around the world.

It's weather is also decidedly New Zealand, with snowfall throughout winter, lukewarm highs in summer, and roaring winds throughout the year. Most people don't even consider visiting. Those that do are usually hypnotized by the natural splendor and leave Australia with Tasmania as their endearing highlight. Tasmania is around 200 miles north to south although that's a winding and mountainous 200 miles. It's shorter east to west. One essential note though: Tasmania really requires your own transport or a tour, as public transport is sporadic and fails to connect the remote wilderness you came to explore.

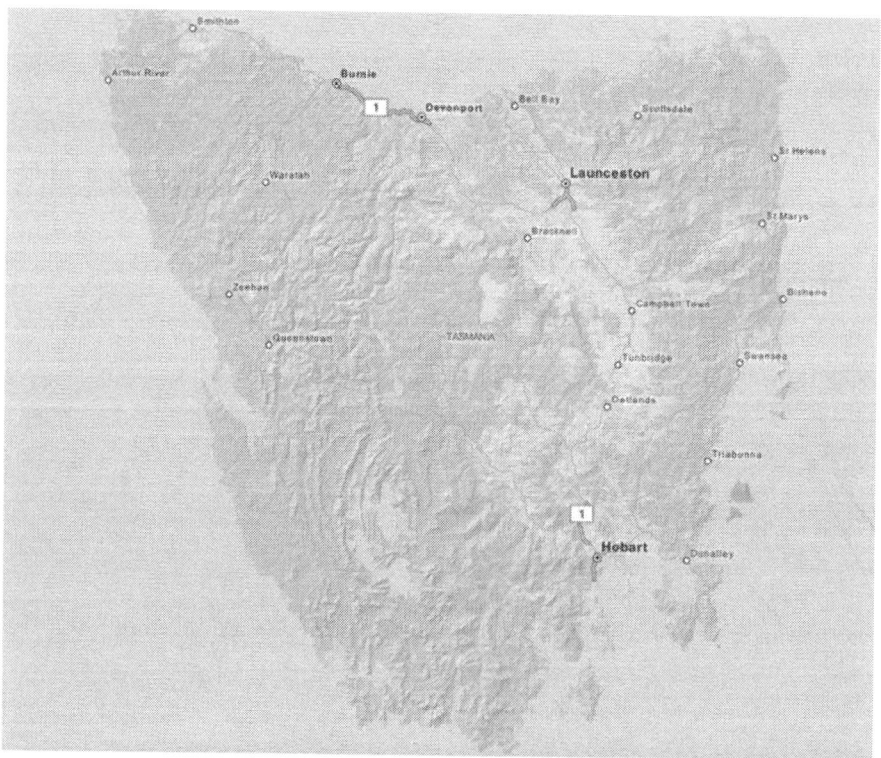

©Openstreetmap contributors

Travel Essentials for Tasmania

Getting Here: Most people arrive by plane, landing in Hobart, the Tasmanian capital. From Melbourne you can also fly to Launceston, Burnie, and Devonport. The other option is the Spirit of Tasmania Ferries, taking the full day or full night to journey from Melbourne to Devonport.

Getting Around: Unfortunately, most of Tasmania's bounty requires your own transport. That could be two legs or four wheels. Tours can be arranged from Hobart and Devonport that take in a spread of the national parks.

Planning an Itinerary: Hobart is the largest city and capital of the region. Burnie, Lauceston and Devonport, are the other cities but the most part, Tasmania is about meandering through mountains and forests and then exploring national parks that remain completely untamed and unspoiled. How long you stay depends on your penchant for adventure.

Accommodation in Tasmania: Cheaper and more spacious than mainland Australia and that's in the towns. Head into the national parks and it's free to camp just about anywhere. Just take all your own supplies and don't leave any garbage.

Experiences in Tasmania

- Capital city **Hobart** is as chilled as they come, dominated by the bizarre rocks of **Mount Wellington**. Climbing the mountain provides stunning views onto the bay, the colors of **Salamanca outdoor market** camouflage stunning fresh food, while the **Penitentiary Chapel** provides a change of pace and a look at the island's convict history.

- **Boat cruises** spend the day touring the smaller islands and beaches that roll around the exterior of Hobart. It can be rough out at sea here and the experience is one of rugged immersion than tropical excursion. A more adventurous option is to kayak along the coastline to secret bays.

- The whole southwest of Tasmania rolls untrammeled under the protection of the **Southwest National Park,** a rarely visited place for camping beneath the stars.

- **Launceston** is a small and cute enough town. Its highlight is **Cataracts Gorge Reserve,** barely 15 minutes walk outside town, a mix of stunning cliffside views and a chairlift across the Tamar River.

- Along the eastern coast you can discover the kind of white beaches that make every friend on Facebook drool. They're not particularly accessible, but with a sense of adventure the likes of **Binalong Bay** and the beaches around **Bicheno** can serve up postcards from the annals of escapist reverie.

- **Stanley** is the base for many easy walking trails and a good option if you're on public transport. An **evocative coastline under dense forest protection** extends west from here, best admired via a walking track or from the summit of **The Nut.**

- Tasmania is a **land of national parks** with 19 of them covering almost half the island. Each national park has a visitors center where park fees are paid and detailed maps can be found. If you're visiting many national parks it's cheaper to purchase an encompassing holiday pass. Always stick to marked trails and never feed the wild animals. For many hikes you'll need to sign the visitor's book, a safety precaution given the complete lack of phone signal. If you don't return, the rescue operation will begin. Camping is easily the funnest and cheapest option and only a few national parks have accommodation. The most visited and accessible national parks are listed below and all are connected by sealed roads.

  - **Ben Lomand**: High and mountainous, Ben Lomand is mainly visited for its winter ski season.

  - **Cradle Mountain-Lake St Clair**: Filled with walking tracks and dotted with serene hidden lakes, this UNESCO World Heritage Site is probably the island's most accessible escape into beautiful and deserted wilderness. Also offers skiing in winter.

- **Franklin-Gordon Wild Rivers:** Remote and dominated by four rivers, a place for hiking, fishing, and getting lost.

- **Freycinet:** Sprinkled with sapphire waters and white sandy beaches, and dominated by a series of harsh pink granite mountains, Freycinet is both beach escape, day walks, and cycles. **Wineglass Bay** regularly tops lists of the world's best beaches, the clear blue waters engulfed by thick green forest.

- **Mole Creek Karst:** Covered in over 300 caves and sinkholes, experiences at this small national park are centered on tours of the accessible **Marakoopa and King Solomons caves.**

- **Mt Field:** Covered in glacial history and more Antarctica than Australia, this green and white paradise is less than 90 minutes drive from Hobart (day tours available from the capital). Waterfalls cover the rainforests and there are many easy walks from the information center. Truly remote and white-tinged in winter.

- The **Tasmanian devil** isn't merely a fairytale creation, it's a carnivorous marsupial that lives wild across the island. It's far from being alone in this protected landscape. **Koalas, kangaroos, and wallabies,** roam free, and it's difficult to spend a couple of days in Tasmania without seeing them. They begin to blend into the backdrop and become as omnipresent as jagged mountain peaks, wind, and clear soothing waters. **Wombats, platypus and possums,** are harder to see, but spend a few days and there's a decent chance of coming across them.

- For an overarching glimpse at the natural splendor of Tasmania, many visitors take tours to the **Bay of Fires**, a mingling of blue ocean waters, burning red rocks, and remarkably white sand. Surf, fish, hike, or sit back and take in the views.

- On an island of such untamed nature, hiking trails seem to start every other mile. The individual national park visitors centers dish out maps for all the parks and there are literally thousands of short and day hikes. The two most renowned multi-day hikes are the **Overland Track** through classic bushland from Lake St Clair to Cradle Mountain, or the almost scarily remote **South Coast Track**; you'll be flown in to Melaleauca by light aircraft for the six day walk to Cockle Creet.

Chapter 9: The East Coast

While Australia has almost 20,000 miles of coastline, it's the 2000 odd miles between Sydney and Cairns that receive the bulk of the visitors. With the Great Barrier Reef running alongside a single coastal highway, and the destinations a mix of cute fishing village and brazen party towns, the East Coast is an exuberant and diverse journey. It's the most popular of Australia's overland routes and the spray painted campervans are almost as abundant as the kangaroos on route. You don't need you're own wheels. Popular destinations have easy flight connections to Sydney and Melbourne and it's also easy to travel just part of the route by road. And despite the popularity, you're never more than 20 minutes away from a deserted beach with exquisite views. This is the Pacific Ocean, so ignite all the images of the tropics.

This section is split into two, running north from Sydney. Sydney to Gold Coast, around 900kms, and Brisbane to Cairns, a further 1800kms.

Getting Here: The East Coast is littered with airports. Sydney, Brisbane, Gold Coast, and Cairns, all have international airports. These connect with other popular destinations on the coast, such as Fraser Island or the Whitsundays. It's easy to use any of these destinations as the start and end of an overland trip.

Getting Around: With enough time, traveling the East Coast by land is a major highlight of Australia. Destinations are more densely packed than elsewhere yet there's still the wonderful sense of freedom and getting lost. Vehicle rental companies offer one way rentals almost as standard and consider that it will be cheaper to travel in the opposite direction to most travelers (see Chapter 2: Getting Around).

Planning an Itinerary: While the adventure is seemingly endless, it's worth remembering the distances. Sydney to Cairns is 2700kms, which equates to 35 hours of travel or driving time. There's only one road along the East Coast, so you'll either be heading north or south. The abundance of airports are a wise option for shorter trips. Also consider, combining flying with an overland section of the coast. Brisbane to Cairns is a longer journey but there's far more places to stop.

Accommodation on the East Coast: The mixed bag of accommodation on offer reflects the diversity of the East Coast destinations. Campsites and hostels are extremely abundant and popular throughout, and they often provide better quality than more expensive options. In popular destinations you'll find a choice of beachside cottages, city hotels, and lavish casino resorts tailored to Chinese tourists.

Sydney to Gold Coast

©Openstreetmap Contributors

Head north from Sydney and images of the bridge and opera house give way to a coastline that becomes more and more tropical. There are numerous towns and suburbs to stop at, although the majority will whizz through and handpick just one or two. The Gold Coast is an entry point for budget airline flights from Asia. It's lies just south of Brisbane and is the next major city you reach after heading north. The following are listed northwards from Sydney.

- Immediately north of Sydney is the **Central Coast**, a stretch of urbanized beaches and suburbs popular with commuters and local tourists. Just over an hour away is the region's second city, **Newcastle**, a rather drab hub that's most useful for exploring Hunter's Valley (see Chapter 5). Next destination north is **Forster,** a popular beach family holiday resort for Sydney locals and the heart of the **Holiday Coast**.

- 400kms north of Sydney is **Port Macquarie**, a more inherently attractive stop for foreign visitors. Whales migrate along here during summer and they can be spotted from the headlands. **Whale watching tours** can be found and nature is also discovered at the **Koala Hospital** and **Billabong Koala and Wildlife Park**, where petting and cuddling koalas and others is possible. Otherwise there's excellent surf and a handful of beaches to spend an afternoon or two.

- **Coffs Harbour** is the haunt of grandparents staying in caravans and eating fish and chips overlooking the port. It was one of Australia's earliest holiday resort towns and that makes it either adorably cute or unbearably old-fashioned dependent on your viewpoint. Nobody can dispute that it's a pleasant stop.

- Many visitors skip through the above and focus their time on the **Northern Rivers** region, a diverse stretch of coastline that offers surfing havens, tropical rainforests, hippie communities, uncrowded beaches, and backpacker filled beaches. With all year round sunshine yet no searing extremes, it's one of Australia's most visited regions:

  - **Yamba** is the quintessential alternative beach retreat, a mingling of surfers, hippies, and lazing away weeks in a hammock.

  - **Yuraygir and Bundjalung National Parks** offers hiking and adventures into pristine rainforest, with the trees tumbling down onto the Pacific Ocean and hardly any footprints to follow. You'll either need your own transport or use Yamba as a base to explore.

- ○ **Lennox Head** is a quiet coastal village with a long right hand surf break, and it's becoming an alternative to nearby Byron Bay.

- ○ With whales breaching just off shore and huge coastal cliffs fringing the town, **Byron Bay** is an almost essential East Coast stop. While its ambiance and roots are alternative hippie lifestyle, its modern facade is tailored to more free spending tourists. Still, with bars and beaches galore, it can be a difficult place to leave.

- ○ While Australia has a notoriously tough stance of drugs, **Nimbin** somehow developed into an anything goes community where marijuana fumes fill the streets and the welcome board declares "addiction can be a nightmare: what's yours?" One hour inland from Byron Bay it's where you'll find magic mushrooms and weed openly sold on the streets and the **Marijuana Museum**. Recommended if that's your thing. A sketchy no-go if it's not.

- Loud, brash, and rising skyward, the **Gold Coast** is indelibly situated along a long and (of course) golden stretch of sand that curves for some 40kms. Some are immediately turned off by the high-rise apartments and sometimes trashy suburbs, others take the Gold Coast for its unbeatable sunshine, surf, and laid-back party atmosphere. **Surfers Paradise** is the hub of tourist activity with busy beaches and hundreds of beginner surfers trying to land their first wave. Walk either way from here and there are over **30 wide framed beaches** of equal beauty and less tourists. Fringing the sand are casinos, family resorts, innumerable beach bars, and hundreds of restaurants. For the best surf, **Snappers Rocks** is where the Quicksilder Pro is held.

- The Gold Coast is theme park central, the options combine typical seaside options with endemic Australian wildlife. The names say everything you need to know and admission ranges between $40 –

100: Currumbin Wildlife Sanctuary, Sea World, White Water World, Tropical Fruit World, Wet 'n' Wild, Australian Outback Spectacular.

Brisbane to Cairns

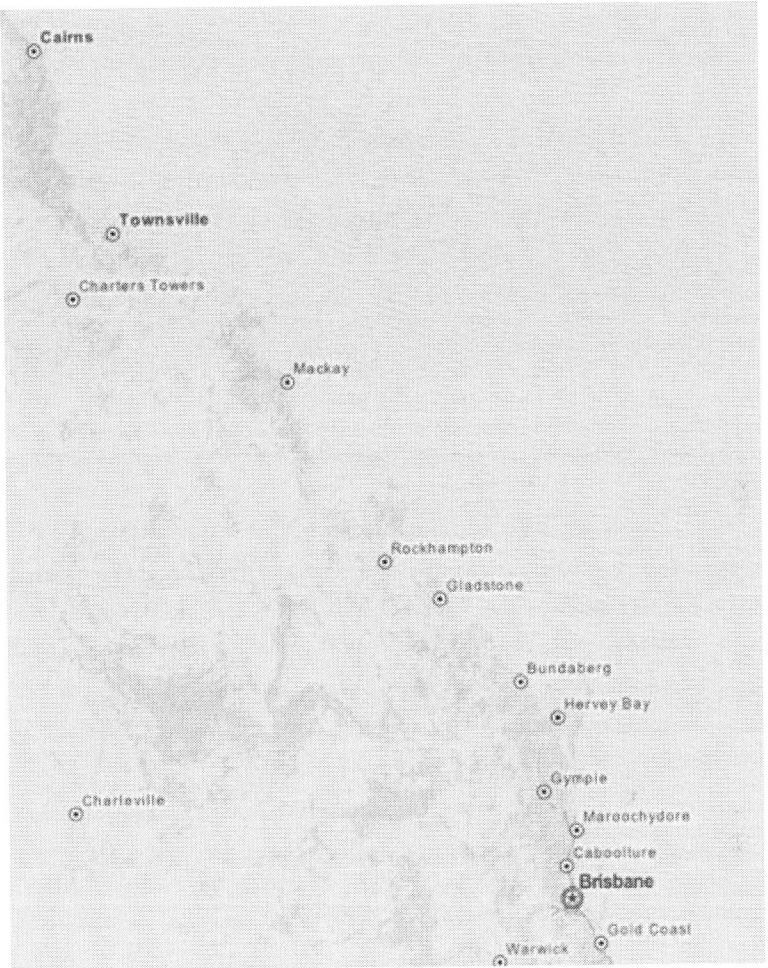

©Openstreetmap contributors

The northern Gold Coast suburbs merge into the south of Brisbane, the largest Australian city north of Sydney and an excellent transport hub for everything East Coast. This region is perhaps the most famous destination in Australia outside Sydney. It's where you'll find the Great Barrier Reef, white sand islands, tropical and sub-tropical rainforest, mile after mile of deserted beach, and easy journeys into the red hinterland. Cairns in the north epitomizes the region; indelibly tranquil and welcoming, despite the recent rise in popularity. From Brisbane, the destinations initially come thick and fast before they thin out on the long journey north.

- **Brisbane** divides opinion. It's a pleasant coastal city, retaining a village like ambiance that belies its size, yet still bubbling with vibrant vitality. However, it doesn't have the iconic sights of Sydney or Melbourne, meaning it often gets shunned by visitors.

  - Wander the streets and gaze at impressive old architecture, including **Brisbane City Hall, four different cathedrals, Commissariat Store, Parliament House and Old Government House**. Then take in the bustling modernity of the city by walking the riverfront at sundown.

  - For aching views onto city, ocean and arid hinterland, climb **Mt Coot-tha. Botanical Gardens** can be found up here along with a variety of **hiking and mountain bike trails**.

  - Keeping things simple for tourists, the **Queensland Cultural Centre** ensures you don't have to tour the city to take your fill of art. **Queensland Art Gallery, Gallery of Modern Art, Queensland Museum, and Queensland Performing Arts Centre** can all be found here, beside the green parklands of the **South Bank**.

  - Brisbane is a love it or ignore it kind of city. Some visitors will prefer its funky and almost **bohemian style**, while others will rush onwards either north of south. It's a city that rewards sticking around and **exploring**; there's always a new bar or venue opening.

- Just north from Brisbane the **Sunshine Coast** offers idyllic glimpses of what's to come. Unlike the Gold Coast, it's low-rise, relatively quiet, and rolling to a cozy small-town atmosphere. There's a whole series of towns and villages that spill onto the white sand, the most popular of these being **Noosa, Caloundra**, and **Coolum**. For escaping and soaking up the beach life there are few better places.

- After the Sunshine Coast the road winds inland, rejoining the Pacific Ocean at **Hervey Bay**. It's a cute enough beachside town, but the airport and popularity is due to being the jumping off point for **Fraser Island**, the world's largest sand island. Sapphire waters lull onto endless dunes, exploration is made by Landrover or on foot, and the interior is framed by mangroves and forest. Around the shore you'll find **whale watching trips**, **divingand snorkeling**, and long days lazed away in dreamy images of tropical beach paradise. Fraser Island resembles a photoshopped postcard, so white and tropical you're almost blinded. Adventure tours can be organized from Hervey Bay but you'll also find tour operators all the way along the East Coast offering trips. These involve taking a Landrover and exploring the remote unspoiled parts of the island. There are also regular boats across from Hervey Bay and established resorts dotted around the island.

- Head north and the landscape flattens out, becoming dominated by endless miles of sugarcane plantations and agricultural fields. Just out of shore, this marks the southern reaches of the Great Barrier Reef. **Bundaberg** is the southern hub for seasonal agricultural workers and is buzzing with young backpackers on a working holiday visa (see Chapter 3). **Mackay** and **Gladstone** are other popular hubs for this as well as entry points for the Great Barrier Reef (see below).

- Within four hours of leaving Brisbane you're deeply embedded in rural Queensland. Beach destinations are small and low-key, epitomized by **The Town of 1770** or **Agnes Water**, two hours north of Bundaberg. Incalculable miles of white sand beach are almost always deserted and the quaint local atmosphere can keep you transfixed for way longer than you really should. With your own transport, every short journey off the highway is likely to bring another stretch of untrammeled sand. On public transport, some of these destinations can be difficult to connect.

Islands off the East Coast

- The next major stop off along the coast are the **Whitsunday Islands**, an assortment of white sand islands in the heart of the Great Barrier Reef. These are the islands that Australia use to market its tropical bounty to the world and they rarely disappoint.

  ☐ **Hamilton Island** is the most developed, with its own airport, a golf course, and a few dozen high-end resorts. It's not a deserted picture of bliss though, more a place to spot those with super-yachts and money to burn. You're likely to pass through here if exploring the Whitsundays without a tour.

  ☐ **Whitsunday Island** is the largest, home to dozens of secluded coves and the renowned five mile long **Whitehaven Beach**. The sand's so white you need sunglasses (and not just the fake ones) and the island's national park status ensures a tropical lost feel.

  ☐ Exploring the Whitsunday Islands is usually done via a single day or multi-day **boat cruise** from **Airlie Beach**. There's a huge range of options and these tours are sold by operators all along the East Coast. They normally include stops on deserted white sand islands, swimming in turquoise waters, snorkeling and diving with unfathomable visibility, all meals, and a picturesque journey through an uninhabited and untouched landscape. Most are two or three night trips.

- ☐ Boat companies also offer **tailored private trips** and there's months of exploration to be had. Another option is to take boats from Hamilton or Airlie Beach to some of the deserted islands, then **pitch your own tent** (bring all food and supplies).

- ☐ A series of islands are home to upmarket resorts, including **Hayman, Daydream, Long,** and **Lindeman. South Molle Island** has a backpacker focused resort. All offer boat transfer from the mainland and the kind of ocean living you might expect of a famous Indian Ocean island.

- **Proserpine** is worth noting for **Prosperine Airport,** or Whitsunday Coast Airport. It's an easy way in to this remote piece of Queensland, with buses from the airport to Airlie Beach costing $15.

- **Airlie Beach** has developed into more than just a transport hub for the Whitsundays. A wide man-made lagoon is often filled with bronzed bodies awaiting or returning from a Whitsunday's trip, and the atmosphere is one of chilling and partying.

- Wide open plantations begin to merge with the tropics as you reach **Townsville**, the landscape beginning to deliver rolling scenery and lush hues of green. Townsville resembles more of a backward country bumpkin town than a coastal allurer, but it's an important transport intersection with an airport and a place on all Cairns to Brisbane bus schedules.

- All journeys along the East Coast are likely to feature **encounters with the country's endemic marsupials**. Kangaroos can be spotted from the roadside, wallabies hop around municipal campsites, and there's enough space to ensure that nature's cycle isn't interrupted. There's no single spot but there's also no need to pay the entrance fee for a wildlife sanctuary.

- 30 minutes across the bay from Townsville is **Magnetic Island**, less popular than the Whitsundays and Fraser, but nevertheless endearingly tropical and home to vast expanses of beach. It's also far cheaper to visit for those on a budget and another starting point for the Great Barrier Reef.

- **Mission Beach** is another immensely popular backpacker stop on the road north, famous for its 14,000ft **tandem skydiving**.

- West of Cairns, the **Atherton Tablelands** come as a shock to anyone who has traveled the East Coast by land. Mountains roll, waterfalls hide behind fields of sheep, and there's a dramatic slingshot from Pacific Ocean to rural farming community. Many stop for the night in a Mom and Pop guesthouse for a change of scenery and pace.

- Some 1800kms after leaving Brisbane you roll into **Cairns**, an East Coast backwater that's been rapidly transformed into bustling tourist town. The popularity is part explained by location; the Great Barrier Reef is at its most accessible, a rich green rainforest engulfs everything, and the ambiance is one of pure vacation. Despite the popularity, Cairns itself doesn't offer that much itself.

  - The **wooden coastal boardwalk** is where locals and tourists congregate on an evening, while the lagoon is where to catch rays during the day.

  - Cairns has a loud and often shameless **nightlife** scene, centered around the **large backpacker hostels** in town.

  - Cairns is the most popular place for taking a **Great Barrier Reef day trip**. Numerous tour operators offer trips to destinations all over the East Coast, including those further north of Cairns (see below).

  - 20 minutes north from the town, **Yorkeys Knob** is an idyllic sandy bay that's currently being transformed into a super-resort casino with some 7000 beds.

  - An easy 30 minute drive or bus trip north you'll find **Kuranda**, a cute village with a scenic old-world railway and a number of craft markets.

Port Douglas, an hour north from Cairns, is a more upmarket alternative base to Cairns, framed by the same canopy of green and periphery of tropical reef. The town's beaches are more inherently attractive although accommodation and restaurants are more expensive.

The rainforest around Cairns and Port Douglas are a hotbed for surviving Aboroginal culture. **Mossman Gorge** has been reclaimed and the Aboriginal run Visitors Centre ensure that all proceeds from tourism goes towards local communities. **Aboriginal walks** through the forest can be booked here, with authentic commentary about bushtucker.

Mangrove forests in Daintree Rainforest

- Cairns and Port Douglas are connected by the **Cape Cook Highway**, a meandering rainforest journey with picturesque hidden beaches and stunning lookout points. Many tours going north will stop for a photo along this road, but you'll need your own wheels to stop at the deserted sand.

- Flickering with mystique and home to numerous local legends, **Daintree** is the oldest living rainforest in the world. Walking tracks tour the overhangs and crawling creepers, heading onto mangrove fringed beaches and circling past swamps. It's easy to submerge yourself in the greenery and just as easy to lie on an empty beach dominated by an eclectic towering of trees.

- Travel further north of Port Douglas and Daintree and you quickly enter a gaping section of wilderness. The **Cape York Peninsula** takes you to the far north of Australia but you'll need your own vehicle and be prepared for some touch unsealed roads.

The Great Barrier Reef

Thousands of individual reefs form a vivid barrier of color along the Queensland section of the East Coast. Visible from space, and easily the largest in the world, the Great Barrier Reef is as surreal as it is sublime. For all the vast scale, diving or snorkeling the reef brings intricate macro detail and journeys into a kaleidoscopic wonderful of color. It's both an understandable utopia for divers and an iconic attraction for those that hardly ever venture into the water.

Most coastal towns offer day trips to the reef. In general, the reef is closer to the shore the further you travel north, making trips from Cairns, Cape Tribulation, Mission Beach, and Port Douglas, the shortest. However, the accessibility makes them the most popular. Trips from Mackay, Gladstone, Town of 1770, and Townsville aren't as likely to be overrun with large groups of Chinese tourists in inflatable armbands and masks. There are also trips from Airlie Beach and the Whitsunday Islands are part of the Great Barrier Reef. There's intense competition for your dollars so ask around before booking a tour. As a general rule, the bigger the boat means the bigger the group and the more people bobbing around the reef. Some of these tours also offer helicopter rides above it all.

The best diving is usually found on the outer reefs. It's less damaged by both nature and nurture. Liveaboard dive trips are pricey yet perhaps the best way to see the reefs' unspoiled splendor. Large offshore islands also provide great bases for diving; Heron Island for sharks, Lady Elliot Island for manta rays, or North Stradbroke Island for leopard sharks. Townsville is known for the reef that surrounds one of the world's finest wreck dives, the SS Yongala.

Chapter 10: The Red Center

Little can ignite the imagination that the thought of Australia's red outback, pictures of Aboriginal culture and iconic journeys scrolling through the mind. First the warning. The red heart of Australia is huge and desolate, home to some of the world's most inhospitable conditions and seemingly endless journeys between settlements. Yet this red center pulls on every heartstring; it's where you'll find the world's biggest monolith, the towering rock of Uluru; gaping valleys and canyons, burnt landscapes, and an inescapable immersion in the Australian outback. Just don't take the journey lightly.

This chapter contains the destinations found away from the coast of Australia. The majority of these are in the Northern Territory state, and this chapter also covers coastal Northern Territory. This chapter also veers into other states to join up destinations that are geographically similar and accessed together. Despite the immense size, there aren't that many places to stop and routes to take in the desert, making this probably the easiest chapter for planning an itinerary. Destinations in this chapter are listed from south to north.

Travel Essentials for the Red Center

Getting Here: There are no international airports but the domestic airports offer flights to most major cities in Australia. Ayer's Rock Airport is the easiest fly in fly out option for seeing Uluru. Alice Springs is at the crossroads of roads across the desert and has an airport. Darwin in the far north also has a good airport with domestic flights and international connections to Asia.

Getting Around: Buses, trains, and hired vehicles, all must take essentially the same route. There's only a couple of roads through the desert; the Stuart Highway going from Adelaide to Darwin (see Chapter 7), and the roads that branch off it going to the East and West coasts.

Planning an Itinerary: The lack of routes through the desert limits options. Other than flying in and out of Darwin or Ayer's Rock, visitors tend to be on long overland journeys from Darwin to Adelaide via the Stuart Highway and Alice Springs, or the East Coast to Adelaide via the Stuart Highway and Alice Springs. The map below shows the potential routes available, with all dotted lines indicating unsealed roads.

East to West Across Australia

Note that there is no direct route east to west across Australia. Routes going east to west stick to the coastline, the most commonly used being Melbourne to Adelaide and then Adelaide to the West Coast (see Chapter 7). To go east to west, first take the Barkley Highway from Queensland until you reach the Stuart Highway. Travel south, past Alice Springs, and turn off at Highway 4, heading into Western Australia.

Accommodation in the Red Center: This is desert and there's virtually nothing and nobody around. For that reason, accommodation tends to be overpriced and over-sought, particularly in the cooler winter months. Many choose to sleep on the road in their camper or cars instead. Pitching a tent sounds romantic but it's a rough and dusty place to do so.

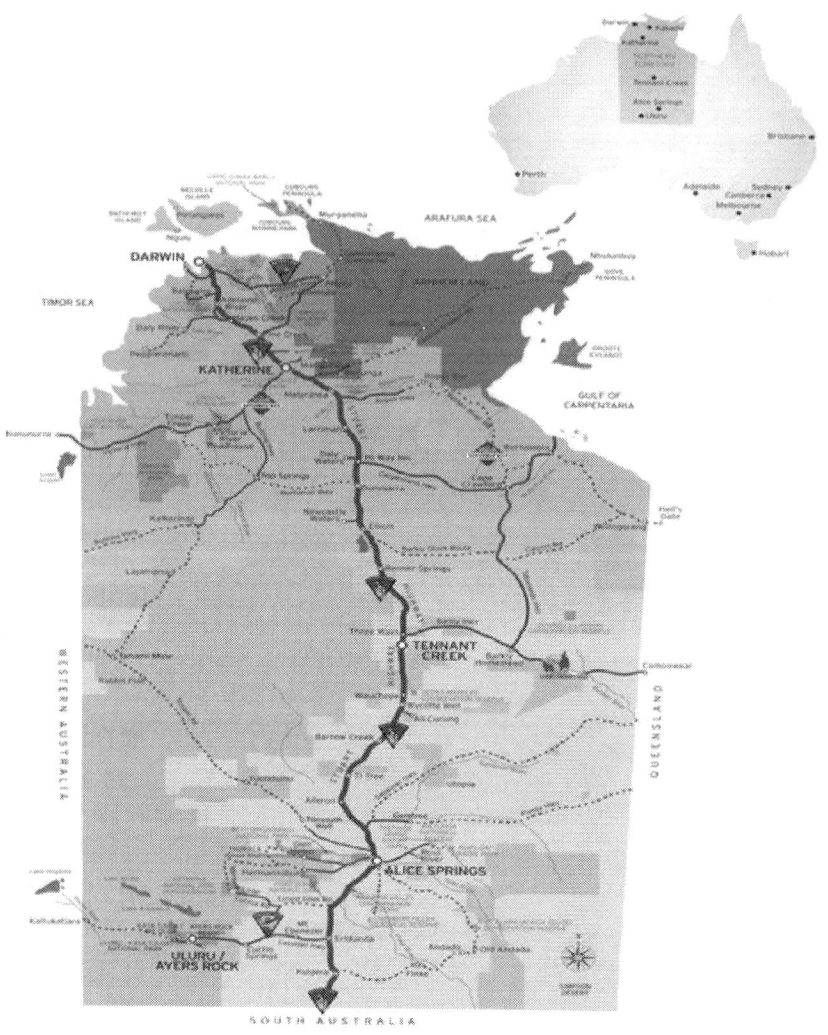

Adelaide to Alice Springs

The Stuart Highway runs straight through the heart of Australia, a pioneering route through harsh hinterland that starts in Adelaide. See Chapter 7: Southern Australia for information on the start of this route. It's a long barren journey, with the first major point of interest in the Northern Territory, being Erlunda, 200kms south of Alice Springs. This is the turn off for Uluru and Kata Tjuta – see below.

Yes, it's just a rock. But what a rock it is! The world's largest monolith might just be the biggest most redolent rock on the planet, moving through a kaleidoscopic color chance as the sun falls across the sky. Uluru, or Ayer's Rock to use the colonial name, is as iconic image of Australia. Except it's not really Australian. It's proudly Aboriginal.

- Uluru and Kata Tjuta are hundreds of miles from any settlement. **Ayers Rock town** is essentially a tourist resort run by one of Australia's largest tour operators. They offer six different hotels, each way overpriced for what they are are The hostel must have the most expensive dorms on the planet and the selection of restaurants is about as good value as a major international airport. The town is ten minutes transfer from Ayer's Rock Airport.

- **Uluru** itself is just a rock. But it's huge and takes at least half a day to really see. Tours leave from Ayers Rock town but it's also easy to rent a car at Ayer's Rock Airport or bring the desert marked vehicle that's been on a longer trip. Uluru is most impressive at sunrise or sunset, when the dipping sun casts dazzling color changes on the exterior. Lookout points are marked and all tours will stop at one.

- A **walking trail runs along the base of Uluru**, journeying past Aboriginal rock art and peculiar geological structures. Excellent information boards can provide a narrative and it's important to respect the signs for no photography at religious sites.

Uluru in mid-afternoon light

- For many decades, tourists have **climbed Uluru**, the single most disrespectful thing you can do in Australia. It's the faux pas equivalent of marching up St Peter's Basilica in the Vatican City, or climbing on the Ka'bah shrine in Mecca. Local authorities are planning to remove the supporting rope; even with it, it's a challenging climb and a tourist tumbles to their death every other year or so. A sign at the foot of the rock politely requests that people refrain from climbing, although the "white ants" continue (see below). It reads, "is this a place to conquer? - or a place to connect with?"

- When the sun goes down you're deep in the heart of the dark Australian desert. The light pollution is minimal and it's thousands of miles to the nearest city. This is one of the world's finest **star gazing** destinations. One look up and you're almost blinded by the Milky Way. Guided stargazing trips run from Ayers Rock town, or you just need to walk 500 meters out of the town to be completely alone beneath the sky.

- Few people are aware that a further 26 huge red rocks lie just across from Uluru, the domes of **Kata Tjuta** equally important to Aboriginal heritage. 90% of the site is off bounds to tourists due to its sacred role for indigenous people. Like Uluru, sunrise and sunset are the most beautiful times to visit. Two hiking trails take you through the domes, the towering red pinnacles casting shadows on the flame colored rocks. One takes 45 minutes in and out, the other up to three hours all the way through. While most visitors come for Uluru, those that visit both rock formations tend to say that Kata Tjuta is more impressive.

- A very popular lookout point offers the prime photo of the **sun rising between Uluru and Kata Tjuta**. It's the norm on many Uluru and all Kata Tjuta morning tours.

Alice Springs to Katherine

Around 450kms from Uluru, Alice Springs is Australia's famous outback town, a dusty and often uninspiring crossroads that's signposted for thousands of miles. It's the base for a number of adventures and the last stop of any size before Katherine, 300kms from the coast and Darwin.

- **Alice Springs** is the iconic outback destination and it couldn't be further from other civilization. It's 15-20 hours drive to Adelaide in the south and the same to Darwin in the north. For such a renowned destination the town itself can come as a disappointment. It's small, dusty, and the prices for everything reflect the logistics of having a town in the heart of the desert. Just outside town the **Alice Springs Desert Park** offers an insight into Aboriginal living while **hot air balloon rides** offer a spectacular aerial of the desert. **Aboriginal Art World** showcases wonderful examples of the best indigenous artists and they run workshops on painting poignant narratives with earth tone colors and bamboo paint sticks.

- Alice Springs is around 450kms from Uluru and many tours can be organized from here (see above for detailed information about Uluru).

- Home to **Kings Canyon**, **Watarrka National Park** is an eroded collection of sandstone formations, precipitous cliffs, and dramatic red rock. From Alice Springs, Kings Canyon is easy to combine with Uluru as it lies roughly midway between both. Winding beside the evocative burning domes is the **Rim Walk**, a four mile trail that really elaborates the beauty; bring water and sun protection, and avoid walking in midday sun. From the bottom of the canyon, the **King Creek walk** is a much shorter alternative. This area is the ancestral home of the Luritja people and there are many sacred sites in the vicinity.

- Heading north the road is barren yet beautiful, passing through the tiny settlements of Barrow Creek and **Wycliffe Well** (a place with an eery UFO obsession), before reaching **Devils Marbles Conservation Reserve**. These mysterious boulders are as bewildering as Kata Tjuta, standing proud in the middle of nowhere and a worthy stop of every itinerary. Most choose to spend the night in the biggest town of **Tennant Creek**, further north, where there's a wider choice of accommodation and some outback pubs that reflect all revered cliches about small town Australia. There's also a good display of Aboriginal culture here. From Tennant Creek the **Overlander's Way** provides a direct route to Queensland and the East Coast. The road is in good condition but it's still scorched red and rough in parts.

- Most people travel Tennant Creek to **Katherine** in one day, the couple of roadhouse settlements in between providing refreshment stops and little more. Around Katherine there are east and west route options. The **Victoria Highway** heads to Kunurra, in Kimberley, and connects with the West Coast (see Chapter 11) while a very rugged road traverses into Arnhem Land. 100kms before Katherine, the soothing thermal pools of **Elsey National Park near Mataranka** make an idyllic spot for resting the legs and re-energizing.

- Desert gorges meet eucalyptus clad forests in **Gregory National Park**, down the Victoria Highway. **Four wheel drive** can really explore the limestone formations, while **boat cruises**head past thousands of crocodiles. From the park entrance at **Victoria River Roadhouse** there are two **easy walk**s with excellent views.

- **Arnhem Land** is the last genuine Aboriginal stronghold in Australia. The land is almost completely untouched by modernity and the area rules itself using ancient traditions and customs. It's easily the most genuine look at Aboriginal culture and it's a chance to experience the world's oldest living culture first hand. However, Arnhem Land does not really have tourist facilities or roads. A journey here is a complete immersion in ancient ways and getting anything from it requires at least a week. A guide is recommended and essential seen as you won't be able to speak the local language; this can be arranged in Katherine.

- **Katherine** tends to be a quick stop off point for trips to **Nitimiluk National Park** or Arnhen Land, yet it's inherently more attractive and cheaper as a desert base than Alice Springs. It's difficult not to detour to Nitimiluk and the sublime **Katherine Gorge**, an immense expanse or towering gorge and rolling river in the desert. A mix of **walking trails** can be taken, and most also float down the river on a **canoe or boat trip**.

Aboriginal Culture in Australia

Worldwide impressions of Aboriginal culture are extremely simplistic. The general notion is of a single group of barefoot people who nomadically march across the country surviving off the land. Before the Europeans arrived, Australia was home to around 250 countries and around 1000 tribes, each with their own language. While they shared the practice of harmoniously working with the landscape to survive, each tribe was a niche specialist. There were spear throwing marine hunters, nomadic desert wanderers, rainforest dwellers, and everything in between.

The most popular exploration of Aboriginal culture comes at Uluru and Kata Tjuta. But don't expect to find groups of Aboriginies around a fire; these were sacred rocks visited for ceremonies and the "white ants" (their name for ignorant tourists) that climb all over Uluru are particularly disrespectful. But all across Australia there are chances to engage, support, and help preserve, the world's oldest surviving culture.

Just because an Aboriginal guide isn't barefoot and throwing a boomerang doesn't mean a tour or experience isn't authentic. Just as they have for hundreds of thousands of years, Aborigines adapt to their environment, in this case, the fast-paced modernity that spurts around them. Ask questions and listen, for they present a symbiotic existence with nature that the whole world can learn from.

Darwin and Around

As the red desert cascades into the ocean, and saltwater crocodiles roam the blue, Darwin provides the indelible blend between red desert iconicity and coastal serenity. It's the end of the Stuart Highway and has a well connected airport.

- The mix of **Aboriginal practices** and western development seems to work perfectly in Darwin. In many ways, the town embodies the Australia that people imagine; traditional and charming yet with all the modern touches. Just heed the warning of crocodiles swimming in the rivers and ocean. That's one part of the country's history you don't want to fall foul of.

An Aboriginal guide explaining bushtucker

- For a poignant look at Aboriginal history try the **Museum and Art Gallery of the Northern Territory**, a museum that brings the narrative of Australia up to the 21st century. A number of 19th century buildings still stand proud in the town and while the river may be infested with crocs, the riverside has some good restaurants, hotels, and cafes.

- Anyone on overland trips tends to stick around in Darwin, the selection of **shops, markets, and sandy beaches** a welcome sight after any time spent in the Red Center.

- **Kakadu National Park** is Australia's largest, a UNESCO World Heritage Site that blends intimate detail with dazzling scale. At 110,000 square kilometers it would be one of the world's 60 largest countries. Waterfalls spurt from forested gorges, green juxtaposes with kaleidoscopic red valleys, wild coastlines hide behind woodlands, plunge pools hang in the shade of gum trees, and billabongs are flooded with endemic wildlife. Exploring Kakadu requires at least a few days. Many Darwin based tour companies offer trips and with your own transport there are hundreds of walking trails and waterfalls to find. The park is home to the greatest abundance of Aboriginal art on the planet, although like many of the highlights, knowing where to find often requires a good tour guide.

Chapter 11: The West Coast

The West Coast is wild and unspoiled, far off the beaten track when compared to the East. While the British shipped convicts to the East and its friendly bays, this side of the country has always remained more untrammeled and uncultivated. Having said that, state capital Perth is one of the world's most expensive and rapidly developing cities, a gleaming yet serene base which runs on a rhythm of work fairly hard and then play much harder. From here the adventure runs in two directions; north, to deserted beaches and achingly beautiful coastline; or south, for much of the same. When comparing East and West coasts, some visitors prefer the unparalleled coastal splendor of the West, while others lean towards the greater number of destinations on the East.

Western Australia's vast hinterland is virtually uninhabited and very few visitors stray into it. Most journeys run along the coast and this chapter reflects this. It's split into three; Perth, the road south of Perth, and the coastal highway north from Perth to Kimberley.

Travel Essentials for the West Coast

Getting Here: For cities with over 1 million people, Perth is the most isolated in the world. Getting here overland means a long long journey from South Australia (see Chapter 7) or a long long journey from the north of Western Australia (see below). Either way it's a journey measured in days, not hours. Far quicker is to fly into Perth's large international airport. A city bus is the cheapest way from the airport (terminals 3 and 4) to the city.

Getting Around: Perth is the terminus for the four day Indian Pacific train journey across Australia. Greyhound coach services depart from here, heading along the coast and through Western Australia towards Adelaide or Darwin. It's possible to use these coaches and stop off a multiple points on route; although at over two days, these aren't the most appealing journeys to make in one stretch. A couple of domestic airports are very useful, notably Broome and for Ningaloo.

Planning an Itinerary: There could be a tough call to make here. Either explore Perth and its surrounding area, or commit to an overland trip along the coast. The latter is well worth it, but you need time – two weeks as a very minimum.

Accommodation on the West Coast: Perth is astonishingly expensive (more so than Sydney) and will test almost every accommodation budget. However, outside the state capital prices can be around 50% cheaper. With so much space around, it's almost guaranteed to have surreal coastal views (perfect for the sunset) and large rooms.

Perth and Its Surroundings

Part surf culture, part trendy hub, part tranquil beach escape, and part fun loving city, Perth's atmosphere is one that rubs off on every visitor. You can't help but love how pleasant everything is, from the sundowners by the beach to an efficient yet laid-back vibe. It's great attraction lies in the Indian Ocean location, the white sand extending in both directions and the sapphire water twinkling from every vantage point. Many visitors wish they could stay longer, but then gasp at the real estate prices. Perth is phenomenally expensive, more so than Sydney, and just a couple of nights out can blow any budget into pieces.

- Wander the perfectly cultivated delights of **Kings Park and Botanic Garden**, home to some 13,000 Australian plants and indelibly perched above the Indian Ocean. Other views onto the city come from **Fraser Avenue Lookout** or after emerging through the greenery of **Lotterywest Federation Walkway**.

- The cityscape is dominated by eclectic architecture; the weird **Swan Bells**, the elegance of **His Majesty's Theatre,** the silence of **Kings Park War Memorial**, the **Perth Mint** and its gold exhibition, and then the boutique shops to be found in **Northbridge**.

- **Northbridge** is where the city's trendy spend the evenings, the extensive choice of restaurants and clubs getting seriously busy at the weekend. For something more chilled but equally entertaining, try the suburbs of **Claremont, Subiaco,** or **Freemantle**. Meandering through the city, the **Swan River** is a playground for indulgence, full of bars, cafe, clubs, and restaurants on both sides of the water.

- For most visitors, Perth's great attraction are the **beaches**. You don't need to look far, the city spilling onto sand that extends almost uninhabited in both directions. **Surf schools are learning to surf** is very popular, as is learning to **kitesurf**, **stand up paddle board**, and **windsurf**.

- Just outside the city, frolicking in the summer sun, the opulent wineries of **Swan Valley** are the weekend playground of many in the city. During the week they're much quieter, and while the wine can't rival Margaret River, it's still a great day out. Tours can be organized in Perth.

- **Rottnest Island**, a $70 return ferry journey away, epitomizes the endemic wildlife that roams the West Coast. Along with the kangaroos and wallabies, the island's beaches bring close-up encounters with **dolphins and fur seals**.

- For those without their own transport, a number of **independent tour companies** run trips up and down the coast from Perth. They range from one night tours to spending close to two weeks stopping at the far off the beaten track destinations inaccessible to those without knowhow or wheels.

The West Coast South of Perth

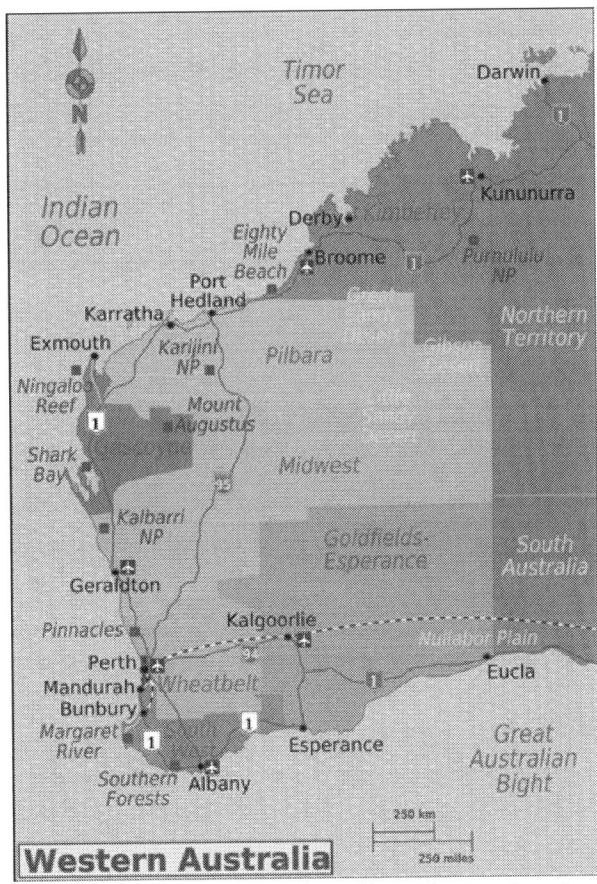

Western Australia

Directly south of Perth, a succession of surf beaches, wineries, and forests, make for easy excursions and immersion in the West Coast's bounty. With a couple of days you can loop into this region and then return to Perth. Traveling further, this route takes you towards the gapingly desolate Narribur Plain and South Australia (see chapter 7). The following are listed from Perth heading south.

- Most people head straight through **Mandurah** and **Bunbury** but they're pleasant stopping off points famed for their sand and upmarket restaurants and bars.

- **Margaret River'swineries** spread over a large area, each long corner on the road bringing another elegant country estate offering free tasting and glorious views down to the ocean. Despite only starting cultivation in the 60s, this region has grown to world acclaim, especially for its Chardonnay and Cabernet Sauvignon. The Margaret

River town is a great base to see many of the vineyards, as well as walking down to the **white sand surf beaches** just west of town.

- Coming around the southwestern point of Australia, the **Southern Forests** bring thick awnings of green to what can feel like a barren landscape. It's a destination for hiking and mountain bike trails, as well as lazing away the afternoon as the trees flow onto the ocean.

- At **Albony** the road splits, two options heading out past the historic buildings of this rather run down town. A half day drive heads directly up to Perth with almost nothing on route. Albony is also the last stop for a long way if you take the road east towards Adelaide. Taking this road, **Esperance** is the next stop, little but a small township on the coast. But what a coastline! Battered by the southern waves and pummeled into majestic shapes, this is a coastline laced in grandeur. If you're looking for absolute escapism, Esperance is a great contender for the top of the bucketlist.

The West Coast North of Perth

Most of Western Australia is north of Perth, the journey along the Indian Ocean and up to Darwin (see Chapter 10) over 4000kms and taking a minimum of a week if you're behind the wheel. It's a desolate yet dazzling journey, with National Highway 1 connecting virtually everything that's listed below. Few world travel experiences are as remote, pristine, or so endearingly sublime. As everything is situated near the highway, this journey can be done by public transport, although the excitement of exploring unhindered may be lost.

- Just 100kms north of Perth the eerie power of the landscape begins to impress. Limestone pillars rise from the sand of the **Pinnacles Desert**, each standing like an ode to nature's past.

- **Geraldton** has a distinct yesteryear country town feel, one that contrasts the Billabong clad surf community that hang in world class waves. Many Perth based surf schools run trips up here and there's also a few options in town for renting a board. Even if surfing isn't your thing, it's worth a stop for the mix of cultures.

- As the Murchison River flows into the Indian Ocean it cuts a dramatic scar of vivid colored gorges and sculpted cliffs. Now housed in **Kalbarri National Park**, this is an outdoor playground rarely visited by tourists.

- Much of the beauty of Western Australia lies in what you don't see on the map; the **cute sandy bays**, the **isolated roadhouse** selling fresh pies, a dusty turn off leading to a perfect right hand **surf break**. Taking National Highway 1 is best when time is on your side. It allows you to veer off and fully explore, breaking up the driving with the hidden spots that might not get another visitor for a week.

- Around ten hours north of Perth, World Heritage listed **Shark Bay** is the confluence of five marine based attractions; **Francois Peron National Park, Shell Beach, Shark Bay Marine Park, Hamelin Pool Marine Nature Reserve, and Dirk Hartog Island**. Wander across to **Steep Point**, the most westerly point on the mainland and the fins of dolphins should be dancing in the water below. The easiest way to get close to the dolphins is at the **Monkey Mia Dolphins** resort. A couple of dive schools offers trips with sublime visibility and Dirk Hartog Island is a real exclusive marine escape. Shark Bay is a small resort centered town.

- **Mount Augustus** also lays a claim at being the world's largest monolith. It's a big red rock in the desert, similarly sized to Uluru yet receiving just a small handful of daily visitors. While it's just as evocative, accessibility keeps Augustus off the radar. It's either a long dusty unsealed drive or part of a tour between Darwin and Perth.

- While the Great Barrier Reef draws the crowds, **Ningaloo Reef** draws the serious divers and marine explorers. Nudibranches to sharks, huge rays to flatworms and eels, the constant appearance of whale sharks...Ningaloo regularly appears in lists of the **world's finest dive sites**. Furthermore, snorkeling here can bring close-up encounters with the big marine creatures that usually only hide at diver depth. A number of dive schools are here. Almost everyone stopping takes the opportunity to **swim with whale sharks**, this being another activity that puts Ningaloo in worldwide top ten lists.

- **Coral Bay** and **Exmouth** are both used as gateways for exploring Ningaloo Reef. Expect gaping wide beaches, scorching all year round weather, and excellently appointed accommodation.

- National Highway 1 runs inland from across **Pilbara,** an inhospitable mining area that regularly takes the prize for the hottest place in Australia. It's not without charm; the ancient red rock canyons and gorges are best found in **Karijini National Park,** a 200km detour from the highway at **Port Hedland**.

- As the road cuts along the **northern coast of Australia** it passes an intriguing mix of ghost mining towns and new mining developments, as well as tiny settlements which are blossoming into beach retreats. Check out **Eighty Miles Beach** to get a grip on how untouched and open this coast can be. **Broome** is the biggest town this side of Perth and the luxurious comfort supplied by the hotels and restaurants sees most people stopping for a few days. There's a good domestic airport here; many with a hire car use it as a chance to drive one way then miss out the long desolate trek into the Red Center and Darwin.

- From Broome the road crosses the vast and empty wilderness of **Kimberley**, a mining focused state that's as remote as anywhere in Australia. Most rush through to **Kununurra** on the edge of Western Australia; continue the journey to Darwin by seeing Chapter 10. The exemption to only passing through is **Purnululu National Park**, a weird expanse of unusual sandstone domes covered in multicolored stripes. It's a three hour drive off the highway.

Chapter 12: A Thank You From Us

Well, you've read your way through Australia and hopefully this guidebook has taken you all the way around Australia. Thank you for reading. Seriously. We're only producing these guidebooks because people are reading them, so without you, what's the point in writing. Okay, we're also writing because we strongly believe there's an alternative to the overly-commercialized guidebook market that has been taking the independence out of travel for the last two decades. But apart from that little moan, this guidebook is all about you. Hopefully it has inspired, evoked, immersed, guided, proposed, assisted, and done everything else a guidebook should do. If it hasn't then please get in touch and tell us why. This guidebook is written from a visitor's perspective, and if it didn't quite hit the mark we're eager to improve.

We believe that Australia is one of those magical destinations that should be explored. Hopefully you're reading this in an iconic Australian destination and thinking the same. Uluru, Sydney, some hidden beach on the West Coast, the Whitsunday Islands, wherever you're reading, thank you again for choosing this guidebook. And if you're reading at home, planning the big trip, then we'll admit to being insanely jealous of your upcoming adventure. That's it from us, other than, try checking out our other travel guides as you journey the most exotic destinations on the planet.

Learn Any Language 300% FASTER

>> Get Full Online Language Courses With Audio Lessons <<

Would you like to learn a new language before you start your trip? I think that's a great idea. Now, why don't you do it 300% *FASTER*?

I've partnered with the most revolutionary language teachers to bring you the very language online courses I've ever seen. It's a mind-blowing program specifically created for language hackers such as ourselves. It will allow you learn ANY language, from French to Chinese, 3x faster, straight from the comfort of your own home, office, or wherever you may be. It's like having an unfair advantage!

You can choose from a wide variety of languages, such as French, Spanish, Italian, German, Chinese, Portuguese, and A TON more.

Each Online Course consists of:

+ 91 Built-In Lessons
+ 33 Interactive Audio Lessons
+ 24/7 Support to Keep You Going

The program is extremely engaging, fun, and easy-going. You won't even notice you are learning a complex foreign language from scratch. And before you realize it, by the time you go through all the lessons you will officially become a truly solid speaker.

Old classrooms are a thing of the past. It's time for a revolution.

If you'd like to go the extra mile, follow the link below, and let the revolution begin

>>http://www.bitly.com/foreign-language-courses<<

CHECK OUT THE COURSE »

Preview Of "New Zealand For Tourists - The Traveler's Travel Guide to Make the Most Out of Your Trip to New Zealand - Where to Go, Eat, Sleep & Party"

Introduction
Why You Will Fall In Love With New Zealand

New Zealand revels in its role as nature's amphitheater, the country redefining notions of the sublime and the surreal. Every turn seems to unveil a new panorama, a new aesthetic seemingly lost in time. New Zealand is unspoiled and untamed. Its status as home of fictionalized Middle Earth is well publicized, but there's far more to the landscape than hobbit holes and orcas hiding in trees. There is bounty to be discovered everywhere and almost every visitor is won over with fresh impressions of natural splendor. With more sheep than people and more solitude than city, New Zealand is a place for getting lost in the midst of the planet's most spectacular landscapes.

New Zealand essentially consists of a series of islands in the Pacific, each distinct and celebrating its difference. Two large islands dominate this definition. The volcanic North Island, full of rolling green pastures and kaleidoscopic color. And the mountainous South Island, home to glaciers, fjords, and dramatic geological features. While the land provides an omnipresent highlight, there's more to New Zealand than a journey through lakes, mountains, ocean, and forests dancing with phantasmal intrigue.

The country runs on an indelibly laid-back rhythm, one that negates the use of a watch and helps you easily slip into the natural spell. You could travel a hundred miles without seeing another person and most settlements still retain the unpopulated charm of yesteryear. Such rurality inevitably supports a famed local friendliness. Everyone has time to say hello and greet a stranger and rushing around is a serious no no. Stress, it seems, disappears the moment you land in the country. Even a journey that traverses the whole of New Zealand will be defined by serenity.

This guidebook has a very New Zealand approach at heart. It likes to keep things simple and tranquil, preferring not to dampen the journey with layer after layer of purposeless information. This is a country that must be discovered. We would prefer to leave enough for you to discover when you arrive. At the same time, the helping hand of a local guide is essential for navigating the best the country has to offer. So think of this guidebook as the friendly locals you meet in New Zealand, full of tips and ideas but always leaving the final decision to you. In this guidebook we detail all the iconic and unmissable experience, as well as all the hidden and off the beaten track ideas that should be considered.

This complete planning guide presents destinations from a visitor's perspective. Rather than use local administrative regions, the guidebook is split into key routes and regions that are easy to explore from a single base. Using this approach enables a clear overview of what's possible when you visit New Zealand, and which destinations are effortlessly combined in an itinerary.

What this guidebook doesn't do, is fill two pages with hotels and restaurants with less than complimentary descriptions. If it's good and worth experiencing then it's in this guidebook. If it's not then it didn't make the cut. There's more than enough enchantment and quality to find in New Zealand, why dilute it with the mundane? So jump forward and jump in to a country that captures the imagination and stirs the intrepidness in every soul. Welcome to New Zealand and welcome to a country that always leaves a lasting impression.

©Openstreetmap Contributors

Chapter 1
Welcome to New Zealand!

New Zealand at a glance

A few hidden islands aside, New Zealand can be thought about as a North and South Island. Cast adrift in the South Pacific, both these islands imbue impressions of trademark natural beauty and tranquility. They're similarly sized, small enough to cross in a single day (albeit a long one) yet big enough to spend two months exploring and not get close to experiencing it all. Both are equally attractive for slightly different reasons. Some visitors prefer to concentrate on one or the other, exploring in more depth and fully soaking up the experience on offer. Other visitors will find additional beauty in the contrast, choosing instead to pick a handful of destinations across both islands.

The North Island has a volcanic history and the lava still spills out of its active domes. It's a green and peculiar landscape, marked by rolls and curves and pastures. Nothing is flat until you reach the coast and dozens of miles of beach roll into the Pacific. The South Island geology is more dramatic; mountains rise in rugged triangles, fjords and glaciers are dappled by white, and there's even less flat space. Naturally, it's colder here and less green. But that's compensated by panoramas that are difficult to rival anywhere else on the planet.

While the atmosphere is one of quaint backwater, this is a developed Western nation with a sophisticated tourist infrastructure. Moving between islands and destinations is easy and straightforward. Roads are in excellent condition (and almost completely devoid of traffic), airlines connect major destinations and towns, and hundreds of tour companies can provide a safe adventure into ethereal landscapes. Hotels harmoniously blend with their surroundings and always provide space (no cramped hovels here) and medical facilities are amongst the best in the world. In short, there's no limit to the adventure on offer, other than your own spirit. Here are a few experiences to get you excited...

Iconic Experiences

- Most journeys will have your eyes lost in a mystical haze and this feeling of incredulity is epitomized by **Milford Sound**, a narrow fjord surrounded by dramatic mountains that empties into the Tasman Sea. It's part of the **Fjordland National Park**, which in turn is one of seven national parks that cover the **West Coast of the South Island**.

- New Zealand is **Middle Earth** and parts of the whole country formed part of Peter Jackson's Lord of the Rings trilogy. The movie themed reverie is showcased at **Hobbiton** and hundreds of other sites across the country. However, it's also easy to discover your own Middle Earth, especially with one of the country's three **cross island rail journeys.**

- Indigenous **Maoris** staunchly defended their land and helped preserve the country from colonial pillagers. Their culture is best found on the North Island and **Rotorua**, a place of exploding geysers, authentic war dances, and effervescent traditions.

- All across New Zealand you'll find **lakes**, each of them fringed by bucolic landscapes and providing the base for both relaxing and adventure. Losing a few days on the lakeshore is part of the local experience, as is kayaking or jet boating across one.

- **Mountains** inevitably play a strong role in most New Zealand experiences. The South Island has a **winter ski season** as well as some of the planet's most evocative multi-day mountain **hiking trails (**in particular the **Milford and Healy tracks)**. On the North Island you'll find dozens of destinations for a day in the hills or on top of a peak. In fact, with literally dozens of national parks and forest reserves, it's difficult to go a day without finding a new set of hiking and **mountain bike trails**.

- **Queenstown** loves its self-made reputation as adrenalin capital of the world. This is where the world's first commercial bungee jump was swung up and it's added to by swings, zip lining, parasailing, and just about anything else to get the heart racing. The mood is infectious, and it's also fun just to watch the ecstatic faces.

Queenstown provides both adrenalin and serenity.

Unique Experiences

- Travel to the very north of the North Island and your eyes begin to cry in happiness at the sight of **Ninety Mile Beach**. Yes, it's pretty much this long, and a wonderful journey that seems to take you to the edge of the world.

- Glaciers are normally reserved for serious climbers but irrevocable shapes of ice are open to the lay tourist on the west of the South Island. **Franz Josef Glacier and Fox Glacier** flow through rainforest and tumble into the ocean, and they offer very unique opportunities to explore.

- **Traveling by helicopter** is normally an indulgence too costly to even consider. New Zealand isn't any cheaper than elsewhere in the world, but the aerial visual rewards mean that it's an experience than even the poorest traveler will consider.

- Take a boat to **White Island**, an active volcano that's still bubbling with primitive majesty. Put on a gas mask and you can trek to the very edge of the crater, where the hissing and bubbling always leaves goosebumps.

- New Zealand **wine** is slowly emerging on the international scale, spearheaded by the **Marlborough** and **Central Otago** regions. A sensual journey through the vineries provides another excuse to indulge in the landscapes.

How To Use This Guide

This guide is split into three distinct sections, each building on the last and ensuring you're fully prepped for a trip to New Zealand. As previously mentioned, this isn't a guidebook that's choked by endless listings of restaurants, bars, and hotels. New Zealand is an easy country to travel in. The locals speak English, tourist establishments are everywhere, and you're often left in one of two situations: there's only one choice, or there's so much choice your mind bristles with delight. This guidebook sticks to the essential information, providing what you need to effectively plan and travel to New Zealand. It's not going to hold your hand and recommend ordering the lamb chops because the burger sometimes comes with too much sauce. It is going to fully prepare you for the country and ensure you can maximize your time and enjoyment here.

By providing a broad overview of everything on offer, this guidebook is designed with the every visitor in mind. Idiosyncratic attractions are included as are the experiences that make New Zealand absolutely unique. But it doesn't linger on the details of 40 different hiking trails. Likewise, rather than list all the different hotels and guesthouses, the guidebook prefers to direct you to the best up to date sources of information.

Chapter 2 is all about planning your trip. It discusses potential routes and itineraries, when to go, how much money you're going to need, how to get there, and the basic travel requirements. You'll find a whole section on getting around and planning your transport, as well as a section on getting the best value and managing your costs. Chapter 2 is also where to come for information about where you're going to sleep and the different accommodation to find in New Zealand.

Chapter 3 is about maximizing your experience in the country and ensuring you don't miss out. What's the local food like, what will you order in a bar, which manners are essentially to know, and how do you ensure you're always safe? This chapter is about immersing yourself in New Zealand and squeezing every last piece of charm from the country.

The rest of the chapters provide detailed information about destinations in New Zealand. They're divided geographically, starting with the north of the North Island and continuing to the...well, it's kind of obvious where you're going to end up by the end of the guidebook. New Zealand doesn't have many roads. Visitors are generally restricted to a series of routes along the country's state highways. Each destination chapter lists destinations geographically along these routes, enabling a clear picture of which destinations can be combined.

With each destination you're introduced to the place and the experiences on offer, enabling you to make a succinct and informed decision about whether it's somewhere for your itinerary. Then the guide goes into more detailed practical information that turn a dreamy visit into firm reality; if you need to know about it, it will be covered in our *travel essentials*.

To check out the Rest of *"New Zealand For Tourists"* go to Amazon and look for it right now!

Check Out My Other Books

Are you ready to exceed your limits? Then pick a book from the one below and start learning yet another new language. I can't imagine anything more fun, fulfilling, and exciting!

If you'd like to see the entire list of language guides (there are a ton more!), go to:

>>**http://www.amazon.com/Dagny-Taggart/e/B00K54K6CS/**<<

About the Author

Dagny Taggart is a language enthusiast and polyglot who travels the world, inevitably picking up more and more languages along the way.

 Taggart's true passion became learning languages after she realized the incredible connections with people that it fostered. Now she just can't get enough of it. Although it's taken time, she has acquired vast knowledge on the best and fastest ways to learn languages. But the truth is, she is driven simply by her motive to build exceptional links and bonds with others.

She is inspired everyday by the individuals she meets across the globe. For her, there's simply not anything as rewarding as practicing languages with others because she gets to make friends with people from all that come from a variety of cultures. This, in turn, has broadened her mind and thinking more than she would have ever imagined it could.

Of course, as a result of her constant travels, Taggart has become an expert on planning trips and making the most of time spent out of what she calls her "base" town. She jokes that she's practically at the nomad status now, but she's more content to live that way.

She knows how to live on a manageable budget weather she's in Paris or Phnom Penh. She knows how to seek out the adventures and thrills, no doubt, lying in wait at any city she visits. She knows that reflection on each every experience is significant if she wants to grow as a traveler and student of the world's cultures.

Because of this, Taggart chooses to share her understanding of languages and travel so that others, too, can experience the same life-altering benefits she has.

22345527R00064